RENOIR

RENOIR

Patrick Bade

STUDIO EDITIONS
LONDON

Renoir published 1989 by Studio Editions Ltd.
Princess House, 50 Eastcastle Street
London W1N 7AP, England

Reprinted 1990 (twice)

ISBN 1-85170-312-8

Printed and bound in Hong Kong

INTRODUCTION

'No doubt it's to amuse yourself that you're doing a bit of painting,' the academic master Charles Gleyre once remarked scathingly to the young Renoir. Renoir, who was at the time a student in Gleyre's studio was quite unabashed. He replied, 'Why, of course and if it didn't amuse me, I beg you to believe that I wouldn't do it.' Renoir's reply was the simple truth. He derived a lifetime's pleasure from painting and his art has communicated that pleasure to countless others since his death.

Of all the great masters of Western art Renoir is perhaps the most accessible and his art the most easily enjoyed by a broad range of people. It appeals as directly to the man in the street as it does to the aesthete and the scholar and as it did once to the American millionaire art-collectors who amassed great hoards of his work in the early part of this century. It is not only that he feasts the eye with gorgeous colour and luscious application of paint; it is also his choice of subject matter and his attitude to that subject matter that gives his art its broad appeal.

In one sense Renoir might be described as a realist. He paints the world around him as he sees it. He prefers to paint shop girls on their day-off rather than heroes and goddesses. When later in life he did sometimes paint pictures with mythological titles, it is easy to recognize his childrens' plump nursemaids undressed as goddesses (on one occasion his son Jean's nurse, the comely Gabrielle, even doubled as the Greek hero Paris.) But Renoir paints the real world and it is a world from which everything ugly and disagreeable has been censored. He is not an artist who wishes to shock, disturb or protest, or even make the viewer think. Indeed he wishes quite simply to celebrate the beauty and pleasures of life.

In Renoir's paintings life consists of agreeable pastimes: eating, dancing, boating and sex in its most innocent and untroubled form. Renoir was a worshipper of nature but only in its tamer and more benign aspects: gardens in full bloom, and the verdant suburbs of Paris as yet untainted by industry and pollution. He rarely painted winter scenes and never the storms, floods and fogs favoured by his fellow Impressionists Monet and Sisley.

Above all it was feminine beauty and charm that proved the most potent source of inspiration to him throughout his long career. (It is here that a serpent has crept into Renoir's private Eden in the form of feminist disapproval of his somewhat limited view of the female sex.)

This description of Renoir's art might be off-putting to someone who was not already familiar with it. It might be assumed that his paintings were superficial, saccharine, or even mildly pornographic. That this is not so is due to the freshness and intensity of his vision. Baudelaire once defined genius as 'childhood recaptured at will'. Renoir retained a child-like delight in the visible world and in his best work was able to express it to the end of his life.

Renoir was born on the 25th February 1841, making him the youngest of the Impressionist circle, though only by a matter of weeks. Berthe Morisot was born on January 14th and Monet on November 14th of the previous year. It seems to be a pattern in the history of Western art that constellations of great artists are born grouped together in time and place. Renoir, Morisot, Monet, Sisley, Cézanne, Pissarro, Degas and Manet, all born between 1833 and 1841, form one of the most brilliant constellations of all.

Unlike most of the other Impressionists Renoir was not born in Paris but at Limoges to the west of the centre of France. But his family moved to Paris when he was 4 years old and Renoir always regarded himself as a Parisian. He was the sixth of seven children, two of whom died in infancy. His father was a humble tailor, for whom it must have been a great struggle to support such a large

family. Although Renoir and his brothers and sisters never starved, they would have had a life with few comforts and luxuries.

Renoir was one of the few great nineteenth-century painters and certainly the only major Impressionist who could be described as being of working-class origin. Though Monet, Sisley and Pissarro all suffered financial hardships during their careers, all came from comfortable bourgeois backgrounds, while Manet, Degas and Morisot were born into the *haute bourgeoisie* which brought forth so many men and women of talent in nineteenth-century France. But Renoir's social origins, however they may be classified, proved no impediment to him; in a class-ridden and intensely politically conscious society, he succeeded in remaining curiously classless and apolitical.

His palpable goodness and simplicity, and what could be described as a certain naïvety, enabled him to cut across the usual social divisions and to be as much at ease in the fashionable salon of Mme. Charpentier as he was among the peasants of his wife's native village of Essoyes. His earthy common sense and scepticism saved him from any fixed political allegiances, and he was able to remain on friendly terms both with the fanatically right-wing and anti-Semitic Degas and with the Jewish anarchist Pissarro.

The Renoir family lived in what was virtually a slum, but it was a situation not without advantages. The building in which Renoir's father happened to take a small apartment was squeezed in between the palaces of the Louvre and the Tuileries. And so the young Auguste grew up cheek by jowl with King Louis-Philippe and, more importantly, amongst magnificent architecture and sculpture, and only yards from the great paintings of Rubens, Veronese and Watteau which were to provide him with so much inspiration.

He showed signs of talent at an early age but it was not at first clear what direction that talent would take. He won a place in the prestigious choir of the church of St. Eustache, where the choir-master was the as yet unknown composer Charles Gounod. Gounod was impressed by the boy's voice and his musicality and urged a musical career upon him. Instead it was decided that he should become an apprentice in a porcelain factory in the nearby rue Vieille du Temple.

The Renoirs' native town of Limoges had, of course, a great tradition of porcelain manufacture and no doubt a job in a small factory seemed safer, if less glamourous than a career as a singer. In any case it proved to be a happy decision for the future artist. Much has been made of the importance of the time he spent there. It may be that five years of reproducing the profile of Marie Antoinette and copying the masterpieces of Watteau and Boucher onto plates and soup tureens helped to develop the fluency and delicacy of brushwork which was such a remarkable feature of his mature work, and from this time dates his life-long passion for the eighteenth-century French masters.

Renoir's career as a decorator of porcelain came to an end, not through his own choice, but as a result of technical innovations which made the painting of porcelain by hand uneconomical. For a year or two he continued to earn a living by decorating blinds and painting murals for cafés before resolving at the age of nearly 20 to study art more seriously.

Art education in France in the 1860s was rigidly formalized. It was necessary for a young artist to enter the École des Beaux-Arts and also to enrol in the atelier of one of the academic masters who had achieved fame and popularity at the Salon, the great annual art exhibition visited by tens of thousands. Auguste chose the studio of the Swiss master Charles Gleyre, partly no doubt because of the low fees which Gleyre charged, but also because

Renoir, *Portrait of the Artist's Father*

his teaching methods were less rigid and authoritarian than those of the other academic masters, such as the more famous Gérôme. The same reasons had attracted to Gleyre's studio three other young artists who were to play a vital role in Renoir's development, Monet, Sisley and Bazille. Poor Gleyre has received a great deal of abuse, both from his own famous students and from the many critics who have written about them. Renoir himself later said that Gleyre was 'of no help to his pupils', and Monet claimed, 'We left after two weeks of lessons of this kind of proficiency. We were well rid of it.'[1] In fact Renoir continued to study with Gleyre and at the École des Beaux-Arts for over two years; and he designated himself as 'pupil of Gleyre' in the Salon catalogues until the late 1870s. Like many avant-garde artists of the nineteenth century, he benefited from the drawing skills which he acquired while enrolled at the École des Beaux-Arts, while disregarding those aspects of academic discipline which fettered his individuality and talent.

Recent reassessment of Gleyre has shown that he had rather more to offer as an artist than was once supposed. Although his more radical students would have found little of interest in the painting for which he was most famous, the frigid and sentimental *Les Illusions Perdues* (Lost Illusions) exhibited at the Salon of 1843, he had made watercolour drawings of astonishing fluidity and luminosity while travelling in the Near East in the 1830s. Interestingly, Gleyre had learnt his watercolour technique from the English Romantic landscapist Richard Parkes Bonnington, who was in many ways a forerunner of the Impressionists.

In 1864 Renoir's first submission to the Salon was accepted. The subject *Esmeralda Dancing with a Goat*, taken from Victor Hugo's novel *Notre-Dame de Paris*, was

Renoir in 1861

just the kind of anecdotal or literary subject favoured by the popular Salon painters despised by Renoir and his friends.

Throughout the 1860s Renoir produced a steady stream of paintings, several of them accepted by the Salon, which were remarkable for their technical accomplishment. They are equally remarkable for their lack of stylistic consistency. As late as 1870 Renoir submitted two pictures to the Salon which are stylistically so different that the uninformed viewer would be unlikely to guess that they were by the same artist. *The Bather with*

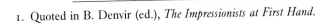

1. Quoted in B. Denvir (ed.), *The Impressionists at First Hand*.

Griffon (now in the Museu de Arte de Sao Paulo) seems to be an exercise in the manner of Courbet with its solidly sculptural treatment of the figure, sombre colours and black shadows. Whereas the *Odalisque* with its exact setting and sumptuous, glittering colour was an obvious homage to Delacroix.

Delacroix and Courbet exerted strong but apparently contradictory influences on the young Renoir. He also looked closely at Corot and the Barbizon landscapists, and at Edouard Manet who was currently the *enfant terrible* of the Paris art scene. The landscapes of Corot, Daubigny, Théodore Rousseau and Diaz were in many ways the direct precursors of Impressionism. Their preoccupation with landscape in its more ordinary and everyday aspect, their desire to record a more truthful and direct response to nature, and what was by the standards of the time a rapid and spontaneous technique were all features developed by Renoir and his friends.

In the mid 1860s Renoir, Monet and Sisley went on numerous painting expeditions to the forest of Fontainebleau, close to the village of Barbizon, no doubt hoping to partake of the inspiration of the older artists. It was during one of these expeditions that the famous incident occurred when Renoir met the painter Diaz. The one-legged and elderly Diaz came charging out of the bushes, brandishing a heavy cane, with which he drove off a group of rowdy Parisians who had been bothering Renoir as he painted. Diaz praised Renoir's work and offered him the helpful advice to abandon the use of bitumen and lighten his palette.

Manet came to the attention of Renoir and his friends in 1863 at a critical point in their development when his notorious *Déjeuner sur l'herbe* was exhibited at the Salon des Refusés. They admired Manet's refusal to compromise with the tired recipes prescribed by their teachers at the École des Beaux-Arts. They were also excited by his attempt to follow the advice of the poet Baudelaire to abandon historical subjects and to show the beauty of modern life and costume. Above all they were impressed by Manet's forceful application of paint; the way he savoured the *'matière'* of paint.

Renoir's work of the 1860s shows the clear influence of these older artists, but it was his fellow students in Gleyre's studio who most significantly influenced his development. The tragically short-lived Frédéric Bazille was the first to introduce himself to Renoir. Bazille came from a wealthy and well-connected family. As Renoir himself put it, he was 'the sort who gives the impression of having his valet break in his new shoes for him'.[2] Bazille encouraged Renoir in his desire to paint modern life and in his aversion to the kind of 'literary' painting fashionable in the salon. Bazille proved a generous friend, sharing his studio in the late 1860s and frequently helping out both Renoir and Monet in moments of financial stress.

Monet was the ring-leader of the group and the most radical. He was already absorbed by the problems of painting out of doors and by the exact analysis of the colours of light and shadows, questions which were to become a life-long obsession for Monet, and a central preoccupation of Renoir's work for more than a decade.

The first picture in which Renoir went beyond the older artists that he admired and achieved something new and personal was a portrait of his young mistress Lise Tréhot resting against a tree in the shade of a parasol. Painted in the summer of 1867, it was exhibited at the following Salon. Despite being disadvantageously hung, the picture received favourable comment. The critic Thoré-Bürger wrote, 'The dress of white gauze, enriched at the waist by a black ribbon whose ends reach to the

---

2. J. Renoir, *Renoir, my Father.*

ground, is in full light, but with a slightly greenish cast from the reflections of the foliage. The head and neck are held in a delicate half-shadow under the shade of a parasol. The effect is so natural and true that one might well find it false, because one is accustomed to nature represented in conventional colours . . . Does not colour depend upon the environment that surrounds it?'[3] With these remarks, Thoré-Bürger, who had already earned the gratitude of posterity by his rediscovery of Vermeer, showed a remarkable understanding of the first stirrings of Impressionism.

During the summer of 1869, Renoir and Monet made frequent painting expeditions to the popular open-air café and bathing establishment of La Grenouillère on the river Seine, not far from Paris. The landscapes they painted there were the first to combine virtually all the features that were to characterize Impressionist painting throughout the following decade. Firstly there was the subject matter itself – ordinary people enjoying themselves on or beside the river Seine, in a suburban landscape, within easy reach of Paris by rail. The Impressionists were the first to discover the beauty of this kind of scene. As so often with Monet and Renoir, their discovery was in part forced on them by material necessity. Whether they had the desire or not, they did not have the resources to make painting expeditions to more distant and picturesque places.

More often than not water was to play a significant role in their pictures. In particular it was the reflections on the surface of the water which fascinated them as the perfect embodiment of the momentary and fleeting sensations which they sought to capture. The special interest of the Grenouillère paintings lies in the technical innovations which they exhibit. For the first time the distinction

between sketch and finished work was dropped. Traditional modelling from light and dark and the bounding of forms by contours were completely abandoned in favour of a bold and rapid technique by which the entire picture surface was covered with broken touches of colour. These innovations were the logical development of the artists' desire to work directly from nature. They needed to paint quickly in order to capture the scene in front of their eyes before it changed, and they did not want to compromise their freshness and directness of observation by reworking in the studio. The technique of applying paint in broken touches of colour not only enabled the artists to work quickly but also lent itself well to the rendering of fugitive effects of light and atmosphere.

Monet and Renoir were not the first artists to attempt to paint out of doors. As early as the second decade of the nineteenth century Constable had painted rapid oil sketches from nature which, despite their more traditional and restricted range of colour, look remarkably like the work of the Impressionists. The difference was that he had regarded these works as merely raw material for the large and carefully worked pictures that he sent to the Royal Academy. Although he was aware that the pictures he painted in the studio lacked the freshness of his sketches, it did not occur to him to exhibit the sketches publicly.

With hindsight the rapidly executed sketches of La Grenouillère have taken on an enormous importance in the eyes of historians. For Monet and Renoir, though, they were the intuitive response to a particular situation, rather than an attempt to put into practice any particular theory. It was some time before they themselves drew the logical conclusion from their own work. Initially it seems that they too regarded these works as sketches for more finished works to be sent to the Salon. Monet wrote to his friend Bazille in September 1869, 'I have indeed a dream,

3. Quoted in J. Rewald, *The History of Impressionism*.

Frédéric Bazille, *Portrait of Auguste Renoir*

François Girardon, *Nymphs Bathing*

a picture of bathing at La Grenouillère for which I've made some bad sketches, but it's a dream. Renoir, who has been spending two months here, also wants to do this picture.'[4]

While at La Grenouillère, Monet and Renoir repeatedly set up their easels side by side and painted almost identical compositions. Indeed, Renoir's composition of the scene corresponds closely to the one by Monet which is now in the Metropolitan Museum in New York. Similar though the compositions are, however, one is never in danger of mistaking the work of one artist for the other. Each developed a highly distinctive version of the Impressionist brush-stroke. Renoir's brush-strokes are shorter, more delicate and fluffy. Monet loaded his brush more heavily and used it more boldly. He is able to

describe a boat with a few confidently placed and fairly long strokes.

A question that inevitably presents itself when looking at the pictures composed with such apparent casualness is, to what extent did composition matter to Renoir and Monet at this stage in their careers? Did they merely paint what was in front of their eyes without regard to composition? Whilst avoiding traditional compositional devices, they were certainly concerned to build up a coherent composition in terms of surface pattern and in the balance of areas of tone and colour. The reworking of the foreground in a related picture by Renoir in the Oskar Reinhart Collection shows a greater degree of compositional premeditation than one might have imagined.

These delightfully carefree and spontaneous pictures were executed under conditions of severe financial hardship. Renoir wrote to Bazille in a letter for which he

4. Ibid.

could not even afford a stamp, 'We don't eat every day. Yet I am happy in spite of it, because, as far as painting is concerned, Monet is good company. I do almost nothing because I haven't much paint.' Monet wrote more bitterly, 'Here I am at a halt, from lack of paints . . . ! Only I this year will have done nothing. This makes me rage against everybody. I'm jealous, mean, I'm going mad. If I could work, everything would go all right.'[5]

The year 1870 began well for Renoir. Both his submissions to the Salon, *The Bather with a Griffon* and the *Odalisque* were accepted, though neither reflected the remarkable strides that his art had made during the previous summer. Any further progress was interrupted by the outbreak of the Franco-Prussian War on 19th July 1870. Renoir was conscripted but was sent to the Pyrenees to train horses, which saved him from the horrors of battle and the Prussian siege of Paris. Nevertheless he narrowly escaped death twice during the tragic events of 1870–1. While in the Pyrenees he became seriously ill. As he wrote to a friend, 'I treated myself to dysentery from which I might have died had not my uncle taken me to Bordeaux, which reminded me a little bit of Paris, and where at last I saw other things besides soldiers and thus I rapidly recovered.[6]

Renoir told his son Jean of another more dramatic escape. While painting beside the Seine during the violent and bloody uprising known as the Commune, which followed the French defeat, Renoir was mistaken for a spy. His 'incomprehensible' painting was assumed to be a secret plan designed to aid the invasion of Paris by government forces. By an extraordinary coincidence, as he was being led away to be shot, he was spotted and saved by a revolutionary whom he had befriended during the Second Empire. Jean Renoir explained that his father,

though a most lovable and kind-hearted man, had a quality of strangeness which excited the mistrust and hostility of crowds. Renoir suffered numerous similar if less life-threatening incidents during his life.

Had Renoir died during the Franco-Prussian War, he would be remembered rather like Bazille as a talented and promising lesser painter, somewhat overshadowed by his illustrious friends. Only the sketches painted at La Grenouillère had hinted that Renoir in 1870 was poised on the brink of the greatest period of his creativity. The flowering of his genius coincided with the flowering of Impressionism. It is inevitable that he should be thought of as an Impressionist even though he later rejected the central ideas and aims of Impressionism, and his Impressionist phase took up little more than a decade of a career that lasted nearly sixty years.

At this point it might be useful to try and arrive at a definition of the term 'Impressionist' since, like many art historical terms, it has been much abused. Perhaps the clearest and most succinct explanation was given by Renoir's friend Georges Rivière in 1877, when he wrote that what distinguished the Impressionists from other painters was 'treating a subject in terms of the tone and not of the subject itself'.[7] The Impressionists did not wish to tell stories or to give an inventory of a scene. Instead they wished to record the momentary impression received by the eye of a particular place (usually out of doors) at a particular time. Monet, who was always the most radical of the Impressionists, aimed for something of the detachment of a camera, that records reality on a two-dimensional plane in terms of patches of tone. This might be seen as the ultimate development of a certain kind of realism, but as John Rewald has pointed out, the Impressionists 'selected one element from reality – light – to interpret all of nature'.

5. Ibid.
6. Ibid.
7. Ibid.

Part of the difficulty in defining Impressionism lies in the fact that the style evolved intuitively, and even when the movement was most coherent and close-knit in the mid 1870s, none of its members was given to writing manifestos. Renoir, in particular, had a horror of any kind of art theory and rapidly became bored with intellectual discussion. On one occasion when he was with the famous singer Hortense Schneider, his brother Edouard, and the novelist Émile Zola, and the latter began a pretentious discussion about art, Renoir interrupted it firmly by turning to Mme Schneider and saying, 'That's all very fascinating, but let's talk of more serious things. How is your bosom these days?'[8] Renoir's question was not entirely flippant. No doubt he really did find more inspiration in Mme. Schneider's breasts than in Zola's ideas on art. Even at the height of his Impressionist phase Renoir was never one to obey rules or follow the party line. He continued to admire the great classicist Ingres when his name was anathema to the other Impressionists, and to use the colour black when it had been banned from the palettes of Monet and Pissarro.

If Renoir had any guiding artistic principles throughout his career, they were his belief in the superiority of intuition over intellect and in the importance of craftsmanship. Distrust of intellect was a constant theme of his conversation and letters. 'If I imagine I might have been born among intellectuals! It would have taken me years to get rid of the prejudices and see things as they really are. And I might have got clumsy hands.' He preferred to think of himself as a craftsman who loved his work. He was equally mistrustful of the term genius. 'Who? Me? A genius? what rot! I don't take drugs, I've never had syphilis and I'm not a pederast. Well then . . . ?'[9]

Monet once remarked that during the Impressionist decade he had painted 'as the bird sings'. The same is true of his fellow Impressionists, including Renoir. It was a period of joyful creativity untroubled by doubts or crises. In canvas after canvas, the Impressionists celebrated the beauty of the world around them. This self-confidence and productivity is all the more remarkable as they were working against a background of extreme critical and public hostility, and grinding poverty and hardship. After the humiliation of defeat and the horrors of the Paris Commune, the public and the artistic establishment were extremely suspicious of anything new. In nineteenth-century France virtually all art was judged in political terms. Whether they liked it or not (and Renoir certainly did not), radical artists tended to be identified with political revolutionaries. Paintings of Paris streets, boating on the Seine and picnics in the country took on a political significance which is hard to understand today.

In this climate the Impressionists found it still more difficult to exhibit and sell their work than they had before the war. Worst of all, the Salon jury had become yet more reactionary. Renoir's submissions to the Salon were rejected in 1872 and 1873. This was a very serious matter, since at this point exhibiting there was the only way in which an artist could make a reputation for himself, and there were very few collectors in France who were willing to take the risk of buying the work of an artist who did not have the approval of the Salon jury.

After much debate and heart-searching the Impressionists decided to burn their bridges by holding their own group show in defiance of the art establishment. This was a momentous decision. It was the first significant avant-garde group show and with hindsight we can see it as the beginning of the end for the Salon, and for similar official artistic bodies throughout Europe; but this was not to become apparent for a number of years. The defiance of the young artists was all the more pointed in that their

8. Quoted in Renoir, *Renoir, my Father.* 9. Ibid.

14

Monet, *La Grenouillère*

show was timed to open two weeks before the official Salon, which they all boycotted. Renoir played an important part in organizing the show, supervising the hanging of pictures and keeping an eye on the complex financial arrangements. Always a free spirit, he hoped to avoid becoming bogged down in rules and regulations, and above all to avoid being labelled as belonging to a particular school. For this reason the artists chose to exhibit under the extremely non-descript name of

'Société anonyme des artistes peintres, sculpteurs, graveurs, etc.' However this precaution was to no avail. Critics were always anxious to discover a new school, if only to deride it, and soon invented a label for the exhibitors. Renoir's brother Edouard, who had been given the task of compiling the catalogue, complained to Monet about the monotony of his titles. Monet suggested 'Why don't you just put Impression!' Edouard Renoir applied the term to a painting of a sunrise at Le Havre,

Renoir, *Fisherman* (left and right)

which was renamed *Impression, Sunrise*. Taking his cue from this picture, the critic Louis Leroy wrote a scathing review of the exhibition under the title 'Exhibition of Impressionists', and so christened the movement. The term 'Impressionist' soon stuck and was eventually taken up by the artists themselves.

During the months that the exhibition was open it was attended by a total of 3,500 people – a fraction of the number who would see the Salon in a single day. Many of those who did go merely wished to laugh at and insult the artists. The critics showed no greater understanding. Indeed the reviews of the Impressionists are infamous. They have become classics of critical invective quoted in countless books as examples of the depths of idiocy and insensitivity to which critics can sink. Many adopted a heavily sarcastic or jocular tone. 'Soil three quarters of a canvas with black and white, rub the rest with yellow, distribute haphazardly some red and blue spots and you'll

obtain an impression of spring in front of which adepts will be carried away in ecstasy. The famous Salon des Refusés, which one cannot recall without laughing – was a Louvre compared to the exhibition on the Boulevard des Capucines.' Renoir who exhibited six canvases and a pastel came in for a fair share of abuse, though the delicacy and charm of *La Loge* did at least mollify some critics. At a distance of more than a century it takes a considerable effort of the imagination to understand why such lovely and seemingly innocuous pictures could have excited such hostility and abuse.

It was no doubt partly the result of a political climate in which any deviation from tradition was seen as seditious. The Impressionists failed to satisfy the expectations of people who were used to being able to inspect a picture from a distance of a few inches and read every detail. When the public of 1874 approached so closely to the Impressionist canvases, they were unable to see anything but incoherent brush-strokes and patches of colour. They felt cheated and puzzled. It seems that many were genuinely unable to make out what some of the pictures were meant to represent, just as a Stone-Age man from Borneo would see nothing more than patches of tone in a photograph of himself.

At the time it seemed that the first Impressionist exhibition was an artistic and financial disaster; but, after having been rejected by the Salon jury once again in 1875, Renoir returned to the fray with the Second and Third Impressionist Exhibitions in 1876 and 1877. The Second Exhibition, which took place at Durand-Ruel's gallery in the rue le Peletier, included three of Renoir's greatest masterpieces, *The Swing, Moulin de la Galette*, and the *Nude in the Sunlight*. But if anything, the response of the critics was yet more vitriolic. The powerful and much feared Albert Wolff wrote in *Le Figaro*, 'The rue Le Peletier has had bad luck. After the Opera fire here is a new disaster overwhelming the district. At Durand-Ruel's there has just opened an exhibition of so-called painting. The inoffensive passer-by attracted by the flags that decorate the facade, goes in, and a ruthless spectacle is offered to his dismayed eyes; five or six lunatics – among them a woman – a group of unfortunate creatures stricken with the mania of ambition have met there to exhibit their works. Some people burst out laughing in front of these things – my heart is oppressed by them. Those self-styled artists give themselves the title of non-compromisers; impressionists; they take up canvas, paint, and brush, throw a few tones haphazardly and sign the whole thing . . . It is a frightening spectacle of human vanity gone astray to the point of madness.'[10]

Renoir's *Nude in the Sunlight* came in for special abuse. 'Try to explain to M. Renoir that a woman's torso is not a mass of flesh in the process of decomposition with green and violet spots which denote the state of complete putrefaction of a corpse!'

After the Third Impressionist Exhibition Renoir lost enthusiasm for such group shows. It was only very grudgingly that he agreed to take part in the seventh show in 1882, on condition that his paintings were designated as being sent by the dealer Durand-Ruel rather than by the artist himself. He had returned to the Salon in 1878 and the following year obtained his first great success there with his portrait of *Mme. Charpentier and her Children*. With his growing success and recognition he was anxious to distance himself from the revolutionary politics of Pissarro and his friends. At the time of the Seventh Impressionist Exhibition he wrote to Durand-Ruel, 'To exhibit with Pissarro, Gauguin and Guillaumin would be as if I were exhibiting with some Socialist group. Before long Pissarro will be inviting Lavrof or

10. Quoted in Rewald, *The History of Impressionism*.

Henri Fantin-Latour, *The Studio in the Batignolles*

Renoir, *Fruit-picking – woman and child*

some other revolutionary. The public doesn't like anything smelling of politics and at my age I certainly don't want to become a revolutionary. To go along with the Israelite Pissarro would be revolution. Moreover, these characters know that I took a great step forward in being accepted by the Salon. It is a question of not losing what I have gained.'

This letter casts Renoir in an unattractive light and makes him seem reactionary and mercenary. In reality he was neither of these things. He was as disinclined to subscribe to any particular political doctrine as he was to an aesthetic one. In one moment he might attack the evils of socialism and in the next question the morality of capitalism. His son Jean remembered him saying, ' "Being a beggar is no disgrace, but buying or selling shares in the Suez Canal Company is." Material wealth held no interest for him. Luxury appealed to him but only when displayed by others and thereby providing him with visual inspiration.'

Renoir was the only major Impressionist to remain living in the centre of Paris throughout the 1870s, moving from apartment to apartment in the poorer areas of the city, and usually leaving such meagre possessions as he had behind him.

Monet, Pissarro and Sisley who had families to support, moved out to the suburbs where life was cheaper. The suburbs of Paris provided all three of these artists, and to a lesser extent Renoir, with much of their subject matter – indeed they have been credited with discovering the beauty and poetry of the area. Renoir frequently visited Monet at Argenteuil after he moved there in 1874. Once again the two artists set up their easels side by side and produced paintings which look at first sight almost identical. It was about this time that the group character of the Impressionists was strongest, and superficially at least all their work bore a marked resemblance. Even

Manet, who also visited Monet at Argenteuil, was influenced, adopting a lighter palette and the Impressionist technique of broken brushwork in a number of landscapes painted in the open air. In old age, Monet told the story of a curious incident that happened between Manet and Renoir at Argenteuil in 1874. Manet was painting Monet's wife Camille and her son Jean in their garden when Renoir arrived and, setting up a canvas beside Manet's, began to paint the same scene. According to Monet, 'Manet watched him out of the corner of his eye and went over to look at his canvas from time to time. He would grimace, slip over to me, point at Renoir and whisper in my ear, "That boy has no talent. You're his friend; tell him to give up painting!"'[11]

In the artistically brilliant, but financially lean period of the mid 1870s, Renoir was sustained by the support of two very remarkable men: the dealer Durand-Ruel and the collector Victor Chocquet. Durand-Ruel was a courageous man who deserves a prominent place in the history of Impressionism. He was a man of high ideals, who believed it was his duty to support young artists of talent. He brought himself to the brink of ruin on many occasions by investing large sums of money in the work of the Impressionists when there was little hope of a quick return. In the 1860s he had done much to promote the Barbizon School and it was the Barbizon landscapist Daubigny who introduced Durand-Ruel to the impoverished Monet in London in 1871, when all three were there as refugees from the Franco-Prussian War. From this moment Durand-Ruel played a vital role in promoting the work of the Impressionists and in keeping the wolf from their doors. Although Renoir later sold his pictures to other dealers, he never forgot his debt to Durand-Ruel. He told his son Jean, 'Without him we couldn't have survived,' adding modestly, 'And I believe he really

11. Quoted in Denvir (ed.), *Impressionists at First Hand*.

Renoir, *Young Woman Standing*

liked our painting, Monet's especially.'

Renoir once described Victor Choquet as 'The greatest French art-collector since the days of the kings – or perhaps of the whole world, since the Popes'.[12] Choquet was in fact nothing more than a minor official in the Customs Office, of very modest means. He had neverthe-less built up for himself a remarkable art collection which included work by Delacroix and Watteau. Choquet intro-duced himself to Renoir in 1875 with a request to paint his wife. Choquet soon became a close friend of the artist and a passionate advocate of his art. With characteristic generosity Renoir introduced his new patron to Cézanne, who also benefited greatly from Choquet's support.

Renoir was the first of the Impressionists to achieve some measure of financial security. A cheerful tempera-ment, his ability to paint portraits, and the fact that he did not have a family to support had saved him from the miseries suffered by his friends Monet, Pissarro and Sisley in the 1870s. By the end of the decade his fortunes had taken a turn for the better, thanks in part to the advocacy of the wealthy publisher Georges Charpentier. Renoir became a regular guest at the celebrated 'salons' of Mme. Charpentier, where he could meet the leading figures of the political, literary and artistic worlds, and find many prospective clients. He was never in the least impressed by wealth and social importance, but his warmth and quirky charm enabled him to get on well with people of all social backgrounds and made him a valued guest of the Charpentiers. Jean Renoir tells an amusing story of his father absent-mindedly forgetting his dinner jacket and turning up to an important reception in his shirt sleeves. Charpentier and his fellow male guests good-naturedly removed their own jackets to make him feel at ease. Renoir's portrait of Mme. Charpentier and her daughters in their Japanese salon enabled him to

12. Quoted in Renoir, *Renoir, my Father*.

indulge his love of luxury and opulence. Exhibited at the Salon of 1879, where it was prominently hung through the influence of Mme. Charpentier, the painting became Renoir's first major success there, winning universal praise and no doubt many important commissions.

In the late 1870s and early 1880s all the major Impressionists underwent a crisis of one kind or another. Their work became more self-conscious and lost that carefree spontaneity that had been such a delightful feature of Impressionism in the 1870s. They all began to doubt the validity of what they had been doing. Only Monet, having put behind him a profound personal crisis, was able to pursue the original aims of Impressionism with increased determination, carrying them to their logical conclusion in the late 1880s when he began to paint series of particular subjects under different light and weather conditions. After a period of doubt and confusion Pissarro was seduced by the Neo-Impressionist doctrines of Seurat to the great detriment of his work. Sisley and Berthe Morisot painted the same subjects, but with decreasing vigour and conviction. It is in Renoir's work, however, that the crisis of Impressionism is most starkly apparent, and it was Renoir who eventually reacted most strongly against the tenets of Impressionism.

At the time of the First Impressionist Exhibition the critic Castagnary had written prophetically, 'Within a few years the artists who today have grouped themselves on the Boulevard des Capucines will be divided. The strongest among them . . . will have recognized that while there are subjects which lend themselves to a rapid "impression", to the appearance of a sketch, there are others and in much greater numbers that demand a more precise impression . . . These painters who, continuing their course, will have perfected their draughtsmanship, will abandon impressionism as an art really too superficial for them.' This is precisely what happened with Renoir

Manet, *The Monet Family in their Garden at Argenteuil*

during the 1880s, a decade in which he constantly experimented in search of new solutions to his artistic problems.

His restlessness first became apparent in 1880 when he used his new-found prosperity to make two extended trips abroad. The first was to North Africa, and was no doubt inspired by his love of Delacroix, many of whose most memorable paintings had resulted from a trip to North Africa in 1832. While in Algiers Renoir painted one of his most dazzling canvases, the *Arab Festival*. In this picture Renoir uses a myriad of small broken strokes to convey the impression of swirling figures under intense sunlight. But although the individual figures are dissolved in shimmering atmosphere, the picture is densely worked and more carefully structured than many of his paintings in the previous decade.

After Renoir's return to France, these tendencies towards a more structured composition and a more carefully worked finish were once again apparent in his masterpiece of the summer of 1881, *The Luncheon of the Boating Party*. The figures are also more sharply delineated than those of *Moulin de la Galette* painted five years earlier.

These stylistic changes became much more marked after Renoir made his second trip of 1881, this time to Italy. It was no coincidence that the artist chose this moment to visit Italy for the first time. He had reached the point where he wished to study at source those aspects of the classical tradition, sound drawing and composition, a strong sense of form and of the permanent rather than the ephemeral in nature, which he felt had been sacrificed by Impressionism.

While in Italy he made a particular study of the frescoes of Raphael and the ancient mural paintings of Pompeii; art as different as could be imagined from his fleeting 'impressions' of the 1870s. He wrote to Durand-

Renoir, *Chloë*

Ruel, 'I have been to see the Raphaels in Rome. They are wonderful and I should have seen them before. They are full of knowledge and wisdom. Unlike me, he did not seek the impossible. But it's beautiful. I prefer Ingres for oil painting. Yet the frescoes are admirable in simplicity and grandeur.'

Renoir travelled the length of Italy and on to Sicily, where he had the opportunity to paint the composer Wagner who had just completed his final masterpiece

Parsifal. It comes as something of a shock to think that *Parsifal* and The *Luncheon of the Boating Party* are exactly contemporary. The guilt-ridden characters of Wagner's gloomy sacred music drama seem to breathe a different air from that of the uncomplicated girls who inhabit Renoir's sunlit suburbs. The artist seems to have realized the historic significance of the meeting and left a detailed account of it. Alas, the conversation as reported by Renoir seems to have been extremely banal and shows neither the painter nor the composer in a very sympathetic light. Despite Renoir's enthusiasm for the Master's 'openness and gaiety', they seem to have had little in common beyond their anti-Semitism. Renoir wrote, 'I felt very nervous, and regretted that I wasn't Ingres.' The resulting portrait is disappointing both as a likeness of Wagner and as an example of Renoir's art. It is hard to agree with the great German art historian Julius Meier-Graefe who described the expressionless pink face as painted with 'merciless psychological insight'.[13] Wagner was nearer the mark when he said to Renoir, 'Ah! I look like a Protestant minister.'

Wagner's name was used as an all-purpose battle cry by the Parisian avant-garde in the 1880s. Everything that was new and revolutionary, including the paintings of Degas and Manet, was dubbed Wagnerian. Renoir became involved in a brawl with anti-Wagnerians on one occasion (probably the Parisian première of *Lohengrin* in 1887). In fact Renoir had little comprehension of Wagner's music and was thoroughly bored when he went to Bayreuth to hear the Ring Cycle in 1896.

The changes wrought on Renoir's art by his Italian experiences and subsequent experiments can be seen clearly in the surface of one canvas, *The Umbrellas*, begun in 1881 and finally completed around 1885. Strangely

13. Quoted in R.W. Gutman, *Richard Wagner*.

enough for a man whose constant goals were unity and harmony, the artist made no attempt to modify either his old style or the new in order to unify the picture. The discrepancies between the left and right sides of the painting are startling. The figures on the right are in his Impressionist manner, with countless broken, feathery brush-strokes and touches of many different colours in the flesh-tones and shadows. The two figures on the left demonstrate the so-called 'dry' style of Renoir's work of the mid 1880s. The paint surface is thinner and smoother, with individual strokes blended together or laid on in careful regular patterns. The forms are sharply contoured and have a sculptural quality.

Renoir's 'dry' period lasted for about four years from 1884 to 1888. During this time he seemed entirely taken up with stylistic experiments, carrying out few portrait commissions and exhibiting very little. He no longer followed the Impressionist practice of painting directly from nature but instead made numerous preparatory studies, often in the form of sharp linear drawings, and preferred to work up his paintings in the studio. From this time on he made many statements about the unsatisfactoriness of painting in the open air, though he continued to do so from time to time. 'There is more density of light in the open air than in the studio where it remains unchangeable, whatever your intention or purpose may be. But this is precisely the reason why light is too important in the open air. There is no time to work out a compromise, and you can't see what you are doing. I remember how, on one occasion, a white wall cast its reflection onto my canvas while I was painting. I kept choosing darker colours, but without success – whatever I tried, the picture was too light. But when I looked at the picture in the studio, it looked quite black. An artist who paints straight from nature is really only looking for nothing but momentary effects. He does not try to be

creative himself and as a result the pictures soon become monotonous.' Despite his return to the studio and to traditional methods of composing and preparing a picture, he retained his fresh, sunlit Impressionist palette. On one occasion he wrote to Berthe Morisot, 'I am going to paint outdoor pictures in the studio.'

Renoir once said, 'It is in the museum that you learn to paint.' Even at the height of Impressionism he had always maintained his respect for the Old Masters and had never gone along with his more hot-headed friends who spoke of burning down the Louvre. Renoir saw himself as trying to continue 'what others had done – and much better – before me'. His study of the Old Masters is particularly apparent in the paintings of the mid 1880s such as *The Children's Afternoon at Wargemont*, which has the slightly naïve and stiff clarity of an early Renaissance fresco; or in the monumental *The Large Bathers* of 1887 which forms an impressive, if not very attractive climax to this phase of his career.

The Umbrellas was Renoir's last major attempt to paint a modern urban or suburban scene. From now on he no longer sought the modern and ephemeral but the timeless, the 'simplicity and grandeur' that he had found in Raphael. The subject that lent itself best to the search for these qualities, as far as he was concerned, was woman, either timelessly nude or else fulfilling her equally timeless role as mother. During the 1880s Renoir became almost exclusively a painter of young women and children. Apart from portraits of his dealers and a few close friends, men disappear almost entirely from his œuvre. Of course it was only a particular and easily recognizable type of female beauty that interested him. All the women that he painted seem to belong to one family; whatever individuality they possessed is subsumed in the search for his ideal.

The Renoir woman was plump and rounded, the shape of her body translating easily into the large, simple volumes of his later work. She had wide-set eyes, a short nose (apparently Renoir even gave Marie-Antoinette a shorter nose when copying her profile onto porcelain dishes), and full lips. Above all she had a skin which 'took the light', inspiring those delicate nacreous passages of paint for which he became famous. Renoir's women usually bore rather vacuous expressions and it seems that intellect was not their strong point. He deliberately encouraged banal conversations with his models in order to induce the expression of mindlessness which belonged to his feminine ideal. He was furious when a dealer named one of his paintings of a girl *La Pensée* (Thought), remarking tartly, 'My models don't think at all.' In his attitude to women Renoir was very much a man of his time, and many of his pronouncements on women would certainly raise hackles today. 'I can't see myself getting into bed with a lawyer. I like women best when they don't know how to read and when they wipe their baby's behind themselves.' Or, 'the best exercise for a woman is to kneel down and scrub the floor, light fires or do the washing; their bellies need movement of that sort.' Not surprisingly he was against education for women and was not at all in sympathy with the growing movement for womens' rights. He said 'when women were slaves, they were really mistresses. Now that they have begun to have rights they are losing their importance.'

In his defence it must be said that he not only loved women, he liked them as well. His son Jean wrote that 'Renoir bloomed both physically and spiritually when in the company of women.' He was capable of deep and long-lasting friendships with women, such as Berthe Morisot for whom he had the greatest respect. Renoir was never a 'womanizer' like Sisley and Manet. He once said 'our profession is made up of patience and regularity that does not lend itself to passionate outbursts of

Renoir, *Portrait of Richard Wagner*

romanticism.' He preferred to paint his models rather than sleep with them. Just as he began to concentrate on the female nude, he chose to settle down with one woman, his future wife Aline Charigot. Aline was a young dressmaker who worked near Renoir's studio, and who posed for many pictures in the early 1880s. She is recognizable as the charming and slender girl playing with a dog in *The Luncheon of the Boating Party*, and two years late as the already rather plump young woman in *Dance in the Country*. One of the things that charmed Renoir about Aline was her unbridled appetite for good food, but already by the 1890s this had rendered her too fat even for Renoir's brush and she had to arrange for a succession of plump house-maids whose skin 'took the light' to replace her as models.

Aline gave birth to their first child Pierre in 1885, though Renoir did not marry her until 1890. He showed himself to be surprisingly bourgeois in keeping Aline hidden from most of his friends. He did not introduce her to Berthe Morisot until 1891 and then in a rather embarrassed and half-hearted fashion. Aline was, in fact, exactly what Renoir wanted – a simple woman with no intellectual pretensions who devoted himself entirely to the artist's well-being.

When she was of no more than pleasingly plump proportions Aline accompanied Renoir on his trip to Italy and posed for the *Blonde Bather*, a picture which marked a turning point in his career. Renoir boasted to his friends that he painted the picture in a boat in the Bay of Naples in full sunlight, but it was significant that he did not render the transient effect of light and atmosphere on her skin as he had done six years earlier in his *Nude in Sunlight*. Instead he painted Aline in an idealized and rather sculptural way, so setting the precedent for all his later nudes.

The nudes that Renoir painted in the 1880s and 1890s

Renoir, *Washerwomen*

make a fascinating comparison with the extraordinary scenes entitled *Toilettes* which Degas made in pastel in the same year. Both artists were referring back to a great tradition of depicting the female nude that ran back through Ingres and Delacroix, Boucher and Watteau, to Rubens and Titian. Both use the pretext of bathing for painting the nude. Neither wishes to present the nude as a recognizable individual. Degas invariably hides or blurs the faces of his subjects, whereas Renoir painted idealized types rather than individuals. Here, however, the

similarities end. Renoir's nudes are removed from any specific time or place. They are pin-ups elevated to the status of high art. (Of course, one might say the same of Ingres and Titian, and of most nudes before Degas.) Renoir's nudes are beautiful and they present themselves passively for the admiration and pleasure of the male viewer. Their poses suggest voluptuous languor or timeless repose and we cannot believe that the towels and combs are there for any practical purpose. They are usually shown in the open air which immediately removes them to the realm of fantasy, as we know that the women of Renoir's day did not calmly perform their ablutions or comb their hair sitting naked on a tree stump in a garden as does the little *Bather Combing her Hair* in the National Gallery, London.

Degas' nudes, on the other hand, are ordinary women of no remarkable beauty or grace. They are shown in awkward, ephemeral poses as they struggle to wash or dry themselves, or comb their hair. The hip-bath, upholstered furniture and slippers locate us in nineteenth-century Paris. The most original feature of Degas' *Toilettes* is that the woman do not seem to be posing. They are apparently unaware of being observed, and as Degas himself put it, it is as though we are witnessing their most private and intimate moments through a key-hole.

Despite his sanguine temperament, Renoir was plagued with doubts throughout the period of experimentation in the 1880s, destroying or leaving unfinished many works. In 1881 he wrote back to Durand-Ruel from Italy, 'I am still suffering from experimenting. I'm not content and I am scraping off, still scraping off. I hope this craze will have an end . . . I am like a child in school. The white page must always be nicely written and bang – a blot. I am still at the blotting stage – and I'm forty.'[14] This was a remarkable confession to a man upon whom Renoir depended for a living. Two years later the situation had not improved. Renoir wrote, 'around the year 1883 I had exhausted Impressionism and finally came to the conclusion that I could neither paint nor draw.'

But his experiments in the linear style did not satisfy him either. As late as 1889 he declined to exhibit in the Fine Arts section of the International Exhibition, explaining to the critic Roger Marx, 'When I have the pleasure of seeing you, I shall explain what is very simple – that I find everything I have done bad and that it would be for me the most painful thing possible to see it exhibited.' Nor was Renoir the only one to feel unhappy about the directions his work took in the 1880s. His dealer Durand-Ruel found it hard to reconcile himself with Renoir's 'dry' style, and Pissarro wrote to his son Lucien about Renoir's exhibition in 1887, 'I do not understand what he is trying to do, it is proper not to want to stand still, but he chose to concentrate on the line, his figures are all separate entities, detached from one another without regard for colour, the result is something unintelligible. Renoir, without the gift for drawing, and without his former instinctive feeling for beautiful colours becomes incoherent.'[15]

Renoir's stylistic problems resolved themselves around 1888, when he embarked upon the final phase of his career. There were no more sharp breaks in his development, just a slow unfolding of his late style over a period of thirty years. A characteristic early example of this phase is the *Bather Combing her Hair* in the National Gallery, London. The picture is tiny but the concept is monumental and timeless. The technique has once again become softer and more painterly. Though the contours are no longer so sharply drawn, they are still firmly

14 Quoted in Rewald, *The History of Impressionism*.

15. C. Pissarro, *Letters to his Son Lucien*.

indicated. Renoir does not allow light and atmosphere to destroy either the contours or the sculptural volume of the figures, that came to preoccupy him increasingly. He has carefully and lovingly applied transparent veils of colour to build up a delicate, nacreous surface that ravishes the eye. Even Degas, who was critical of Renoir's late work, would, according the dealer Ambroise Vollard, pass his hand 'amorously over the surface of such a picture, exclaiming "Lord, what a lovely texture!"'

Such luminous effects were achieved simply, with a very restricted palette. According to his son Jean, Renoir used only eight to ten colours which were 'ranged in neat little mounds around the edge of his scrupulously clean palette'. Renoir himself made his style sound deceptively simple. 'I arrange my subject as I want it, then I go ahead and paint it, like a child. I want a red to be sonorous, to sound like a bell; if it doesn't turn out that way, I put more reds or other colours till I get it. I am no cleverer than that. I have no rules and no methods; any one can look at my materials or watch how I paint – he will see that I have no secrets. I look at a nude; there are myriads of tiny tints. I must find the ones that will make the flesh on my canvas live and quiver.'

Jean Renoir has described his father's late working methods in more detail. He would paint on a white ground, which might have been prepared by the young Jean from flake white mixed with one-third linseed oil and two-thirds turpentine. Renoir began with what he called the 'juice', paint that was so diluted that it ran down the canvas. With this he would very rapidly cover almost the whole surface, establishing the overall tonality of the picture. What happened then is best left in the words of his son who watched him so often. 'He would begin with little pink or blue strokes which would then be intermingled with burnt sienna, all perfectly balanced. As a rule Naples yellow and madder red were applied in the later stages. Ivory black came last of all. He never proceeded by direct or angular strokes. His method was round, so to speak, and in curves, as if he were following the contour of a young breast. "There is no such thing as a straight line in Nature." At no time was there any sign of imbalance. From the first brush-strokes the canvas remained in perfect equilibrium. Renoir's problem was, perhaps, to penetrate his subject without losing the freshness of the first impact. Finally, out of the mist the body of the model or the outlines of a landscape would emerge, as on a photographic plate immersed in a developing bath. Certain features, totally neglected in the beginning, took on their proper importance.'

In his later years, the sonorous reds became more and more dominant. Renoir's preference for warm colours had always been noticeable even during his Impressionist period; though it seems that the reds he used in some paintings of the mid 1870s, such as *The Swing* and *Moulin de la Galette*, faded, leaving paintings more blue than he intended.

Although he was more settled, both artistically and in his private life, Renoir continued to travel restlessly throughout the 1890s; going to Madrid to admire Velazquez in 1892, to Amsterdam to see a Rembrandt exhibition in 1898, and making numerous painting expeditions to Aix-en-Provence, La Rochelle, Pont Aven, Dieppe and many other places in France. He also continued to move from house to house as he had done earlier in his career. In 1890 the painter and his family moved into the poetically named Château des Brouillards high up on the Butte de Montmartre, of which Jean Renoir has written so vividly. But even the magnificent views and the charming overgrown park of the former Château could not keep Renoir there for more than a few years.

He moved three times more in Paris, to rue La Rochefoucauld, rue Caulaincourt and finally to boulevard

Degas, *After the Bath, Woman Drying Herself*

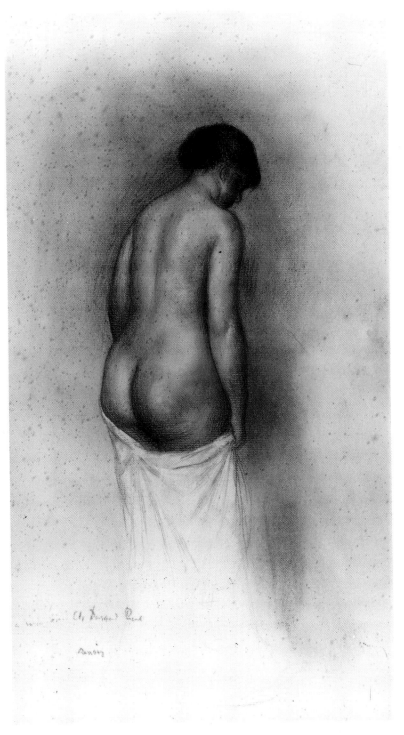

Renoir, *Study of a Nude Woman*

Rochechouart. In addition he bought a house in his wife's native village of Essoyes in Burgundy where they would usually spend the summer months until he built the substantial house of Les Collettes near the village of Cagnes in 1908. Even after this he still felt the need for change from time to time and rented an apartment in Nice.

During these years his household increased substantially. After Pierre two more sons were born, Jean in 1894, and Claude in 1901. Nursemaids were hired to look after the children, young girls whose skin 'took the light' and who also doubled as models. The longest-lasting of these was Gabrielle Renard, a cousin of Aline Renoir, who was taken on at the age of 14, shortly before Jean was born, and remained as part of the family for twenty years, posing for many charming pictures with young Jean.

After Gabrielle, the model who posed for Renoir most often was Marie Dupuis, known as La Boulangère. According to Jean Renoir, 'Heaven had blessed her with two outstanding gifts; the ability to pose divinely and to fry potatoes divinely. She was of medium height and had a fair complexion, somewhat pale, with a few freckles, a turned-up nose, full lips, little feet and a round, soft body, agreeably filled out.' In other words she was the perfect model for Renoir. Just as the servants were pressed into service as models, so the girls hired as models might find themselves doing housework. 'They would step down from being Venus on Olympus to pressing trousers and mending socks.' Renoir always maintained a good-humoured and affectionate relationship with his models, unlike Degas who was notoriously rude and difficult.

The births of Renoir's sons were well spaced and provided him with child models over a period of twenty-five years. Throughout his career children always brought out the most attractive qualities of his art. Unlike many

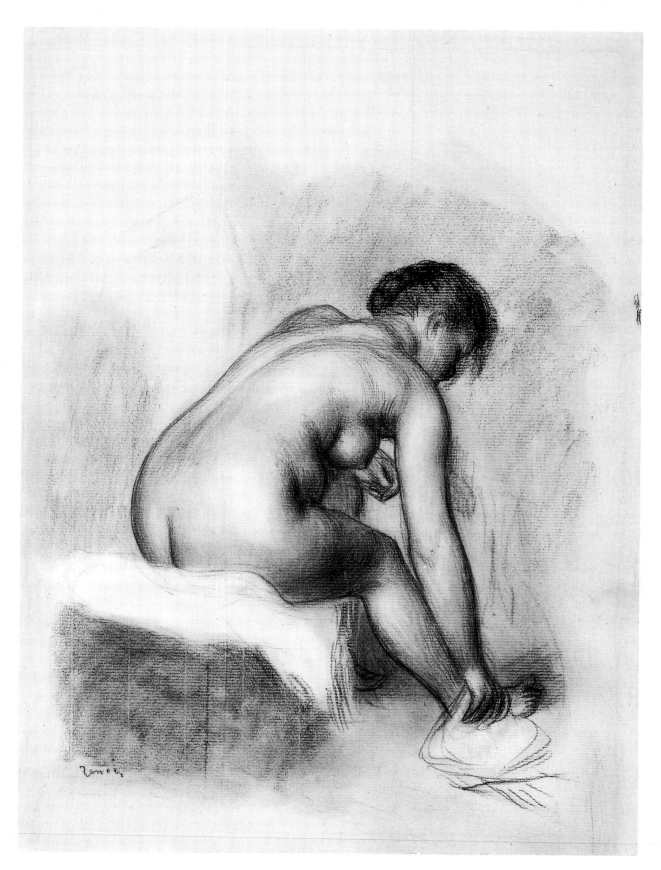

Renoir, *Nude Woman*

great men, Renoir was a loving, if somewhat over-protective father. He constantly worried about the danger of accidents to his children, insisting that floors should be left unpolished to prevent falls, and that the boys' hair should be left long to protect their heads from blows. The long hours of posing were not such as ordeal as they might have been because Renoir did not insist upon absolute stillness, and allowed his child models to chat and play. When stillness was required for a particular detail, Gabrielle would read aloud from Hans Andersen's *Tales*.

Although Renoir was chiefly preoccupied by the human figure after the mid 1880s, he continued to paint still lifes, flower pieces and the occasional landscape. Still lifes were easily saleable and Renoir painted a great many when models were unavailable, and in the gaps between working on more elaborate and ambitious works. Many of the still lifes Renoir painted in later years are slight and rather mediocre, and they make a depressing sight when they come up for sale in quantity in the major auction houses. In 1901 Renoir told Durand-Ruel, 'if I sold only good things, I should die of hunger.' But financial need is certainly not the chief reason for the artist's overproduction. By 1901 he was a wealthy man, and he had never been particularly concerned with money. It was simply that he painted compulsively as if it were the only reason for his existence. Vollard pointed out that whether on holiday or not he still painted during the hours of daylight, and any pastime that would take him away from this routine was of no interest to him.

Renoir painted flowers as a form of relaxation. He told his friend Georges Rivière, 'when I paint flowers, my mind has a rest. I do not make the same mental effort with them as when I am face to face with a model. When I paint flowers, I put different shades of colour and try out some bold tonal values, without worrying about spoiling a canvas. I wouldn't dare do that with a person for fear that I might make a mess of it all. And this experience which I get from these experiments can then be applied to the other pictures.'

The relatively few landscapes that he painted after turning away from Impressionism throw an interesting light on his relationship with Cézanne. As a rule Renoir did not appreciate artists whose work was more advanced than his own. (He showed no understanding of the work of Gauguin, Bonnard and Matisse.) But he was warmly enthusiastic about the work of Cézanne when even the most enlightened art-lovers found it hard to understand. When Vollard first showed Cézanne's work in 1895, Pissarro wrote to his son 'My enthusiasm was nothing compared to Renoir's . . . As Renoir said so well, these paintings have I-do-not-know-what quality, like the things of Pompeii, so crude and so admirable!' Cézanne in turn once said that the only two contemporary artists he did not despise were Renoir and Monet. Renoir and Cézanne enjoyed each other's company and painted together on many occasions. Their paintings are never as close in style as those of Renoir and Monet in the 1870s, but the influence of Cézanne is clearly apparent in paintings such as Renoir's *La Roche-Guyon* painted around 1885, in which he adopted the short parallel diagonal brush-strokes of Cézanne.

At the end of his life Renoir painted a number of fine pictures of the olive groves and the old farmhouse on his estate at Les Collettes. He had constructed for himself a glassed-in shed which let in the daylight on all sides. It protected him from the treachery of the weather and also enabled him to control the light if necessary by means of cotton curtains, so resolving some of the problems of painting in the open air which had worried him since the 1880s.

It was a cruel irony that as Renoir began to achieve

Renoir with Andrée Hessling, wife of Jean Renoir

satisfaction in his private life and his art, he should have been afflicted by an illness which was to turn the end of his life into a slow martyrdom. He first suffered a painful attack of rheumatism in 1888 after catching a chill. The onset of rheumatoid arthritis was hastened by a fall from a bicycle which broke an arm in 1897. From this moment the progress of the disease was inexorable despite the efforts of numerous doctors, including a famous specialist brought from Vienna by the dealer Bernheim. Year by year he became more emaciated and his face and hands more contorted, taking on an appearance that alarmed many of his visitors. By the early 1900s he was walking with difficulty and after 1910 he was entirely confined to a wheel-chair. Many people have left accounts of his claw-like hands in his final years, so distorted that he was no longer able to pick up a brush. His skin had become so delicate that he needed a small piece of cloth to protect his hands from contact with the brush. Although his style certainly became broader and coarser, his eye and his painting skills remained unaffected to an astonishing degree.

The increasing recognition which he enjoyed during these years may have compensated to some small extent for the pain he suffered. In April 1892 the French state bought its first painting by Renoir, one of several versions of *Young Girls at the Piano*. Renoir fretted over the choice of this picture, convincing himself that he had overworked it and that the state had chosen the worst version. A month later in May 1892 a major retrospective of his work held at Durand-Ruel's gallery was warmly received and confirmed Renoir's reputation in Parisian art circles, thereby pushing up his prices.

In 1894, on the death of the artist Caillebotte (who has become better known for his collection of paintings by his Impressionist friends than for his own fine work), several of Renoir's most celebrated canvases entered the Musée

Renoir's house at Les Collettes

de Luxembourg, including *The Swing, Moulin de la Galette* and *Nude in the Sunlight*. The acceptance of Caillebotte's bequest to the nation was bitterly contested by conservative factions led by the academic painter Gérôme, who protested 'For the Government to accept such filth, there would have to be a great moral slackening.' A compromise was reached whereby the 'best' paintings were accepted by the Museum. It is indicative of Renoir's relatively high standing that six of the eight paintings by him in the bequest were taken, whereas only half the Monets, seven of the eighteen Pissarros and two of the five Cézannes were accepted.

Despite his deep misgivings, Renoir was persuaded to accept the Légion d'Honneur in 1900. His reputation outside France was also growing rapidly. Durand-Ruel had been exhibiting his works in New York since the 1880s, and the Americans were very quick to appreciate the qualities of his art. At an auction in 1907 Durand-Ruel acquired the portrait of Mme. Charpentier and her children for the Metropolitan Museum in New York for the vast sum of 84,000 francs. German museums too were anxious to acquire paintings by Renoir despite the

Renoir at Les Collettes, Cagnes, with his model,
Gabrielle, on his left

hostility of Kaiser Wilhelm II to modern French art. The National Gallery in Berlin bought their first Renoir in 1896 and museums in Cologne, Bremen and Frankfurt soon followed suit. Even the English who had shown themselves to be especially conservative and insular as far as French painting was concerned, were unable to resist any longer when fifty-nine paintings by Renoir were shown at the Grafton Galleries in 1905.

Renoir's reaction to his success was one of studied indifference. In 1909 he wrote to Durand-Ruel, 'I am pleased to hear that the collectors are more forthcoming. Better late than never. But that will not stop me going on as I have always done, just as though nothing had happened.' Nevertheless he cannot have failed to have been touched when in 1917 his *Umbrellas* was first hung in the London National Gallery; a hundred British artists signed a letter to him which declared 'From the moment your picture was hung among the famous works of the Old Masters, we had the joy of recognising that one of our contemporaries had taken at once his place among the Great Masters of the European tradition.'

There were also less agreeable consequences of Renoir's fame. One was that his work was already being extensively faked during his lifetime. His highly distinctive style was of course easy to imitate. Jean Renoir tells the touching story of Renoir repainting pictures for people who had bought fakes. Another irksome effect of success was that he was frequently pestered by rich society women to paint their portraits. In fact he was not cut out to be the Sargent of France. His commissioned portraits of women tend to be bland and monotonous. Many of the finest portraits of his later years were of his dealers the Durand-Ruels, the Bernheims and Ambroise Vollard.

Despite his dislike of art being used for financial speculation he was deeply grateful to these dealers for supporting him and promoting his reputation. They were not just business associates to him but part of his inner circle of friends. According to Jean Renoir, Georges Durand-Ruel (who was his godfather) and his brother Joseph were regarded by Renoir almost as his own sons. His affection for them and for their father Paul can be seen in the portraits he made of them, which are among the most sympathetic of his male portraits.

Ambroise Vollard, who also became very much one of the family, was one of the most colourful and interesting personalities to come into Renoir's life in his later years. Vollard first introduced himself to the artist in 1895. Renoir was taken with his indolent manner and exotic appearance. Vollard reminded him, he said, of Othello, and then later, as he grew older, of 'Masinissa, King of Numidia'. Searching for an appropriately magnificent costume in which to paint Vollard, Renoir hit upon the idea of painting him dressed as a toreador for his portrait of 1917.

It was Vollard's suggestion that Renoir take up sculpture in the summer of 1913, an unexpected proposal to make to a painter whose hands were so deformed he could no longer pick up a brush, but an inspired one, as Renoir's paintings had shown powerfully sculptural qualities since the 1880s. 'When Vollard first mentioned sculpture', Renoir wrote, 'I told him to go to the devil, but on reflection I let myself be persuaded.' A young Spanish sculptor called Richard Guino, a former pupil of Maillol, was hired by Vollard to translate sketches made by Renoir into sculptural form. Renoir sitting close by in his wheelchair gave detailed instructions to the sculptor as he worked. 'Take a bit off there . . . a little more – that's right! This should be rounder, fuller . . . !'

Renoir always had very definite ideas on sculpture. The Fontaine des Innocents by the sixteenth-century French sculptor Goujon, which he had admired as a

Renoir, *Venus Victorious*

young worker in the nearby porcelain factory, had been one of his earliest and greatest inspirations – but when he went to Italy in the 1880s he had been irritated by the virtuosity of Michelangelo and Bernini. He believed that Degas was the only great sculptor in the nineteenth century. He disliked the pretentiousness and pathos of Rodin and his excessive dependency upon the model, describing a bust of Rodin's as 'smelling of armpit'. He criticized the contemporary sculpture exhibited in the Luxembourg Museum as too restless and melodramatic. 'You almost want to say to those dying soldiers and screaming mothers, "Do be quiet; get yourself a chair and sit down."' He felt that 'sculpture should be eternal as the material it is created out of.' The timeless serenity and simplified classicism of his sculpture was in tune with the younger generation of sculptors who were reacting against the work of Rodin, which they saw as literary and overemotional and betraying the essential nature of the medium.

Renoir's final years were saddened not only by the merciless progress of his disease but by the death of his beloved wife Aline in 1915, and by the outbreak of the First World War. His sons Pierre and Jean, for whose safety he had always been so anxious, both fought and were severely wounded. But for Renoir art remained as a means of escape from pain and sorrow. In 1910 he wrote to the young painter Albert André, 'Happy painting which, very late in life gives you illusions and sometimes joy.' The Great War was never allowed to cast a shadow on Renoir's art. As he said, 'For me a picture . . . should be something likeable, joyous and pretty – yes, pretty. There are enough ugly things in life for us not to add to them.'

Day by day, as Renoir became more frail and emaciated, his paintings became more joyous, vital and sensual and the touch of his brush more fluid and bold. When a young journalist, shocked by the appearance of Renoir's hands, asked how he managed to paint, Renoir answered, 'I paint with my prick'. This was not meant facetiously. It was a cruder way of putting something he had said before: 'It's with my brush that I make love.' The gloriously sublimated sensuality of his late work found its most powerful and monumental expression in his final masterpiece *Bathers*, in which for the last time he tried to capture that 'state of grace which comes from contemplating God's most beautiful creation, the human body'.

On the last day of his life he painted a picture of anemones. As he put aside his brush for the last time, he was heard to murmur 'I think I am begining to understand something about it.'

PATRICK BADE
LONDON, MARCH 1989

Renoir at Les Collettes, Cagnes

THE PLATES

Portrait of Mademoiselle Romaine Lacaux, 1864

This charming canvas was painted shortly after Renoir had left the studio of Gleyre and in the same year in which he exhibited at the Salon for the first time. The cool, silvery range of colours betrays Renoir's love of Corot's work at this early stage in his career, and the broad handling of paint and bold contrasts of tone show his awareness of the art of Manet, who had attained nationally and seized the leadership of the more progressive French artists the previous year, when his *Déjeuner sur l'herbe* was exhibited at the Salon des Refusés.

However, the trembling, almost feminine delicacy of this picture is entirely Renoir's own. Throughout his career Renoir was particularly responsive to the charm of children, which he was able to convey with a tenderness entirely free of sentimentality. Romaine Lacaux was the daughter of a manufacturer of terracotta products who had perhaps come into contact with Renoir through his contract work as a painter of porcelain.

Renoir painted flowers throughout his career, until the last day of his life. He told his friend that flower painting was a form of mental relaxation for him. 'I do not need the concentration that I need when I am faced with a model. When I am painting flowers I can experiment boldly with tones and values without worrying about destroying the whole painting. I would not dare to do that with a figure because I would be afraid of spoiling everything. The experience I gain from these experiments can then be applied to my painting.'

The predominance of sombre earth colours is reminiscent of the still lifes of Courbet, but the thin, scratchy application of paint is closer to the work of Fantin-Latour who made a speciality of such flower pieces.

The Inn at Mother Antony's, 1866

The Inn at Mother Antony's evokes the simple pleasures and carefree, Bohemian life-style of impoverished young artists which had already been celebrated in Murger's novel of 1848 and which were to have their final apotheosis in Puccini's opera *La Bohème*. Late in life Renoir looked back on this picture and the times that inspired it through a veil of nostalgia. He told the dealer Vallord, '*The Inn at Mother Antony's* is one of my pictures that I remember with most pleasure. It is not that I find the painting itself particularly exciting, but it does remind me of a good old Mother Antony and her inn in Marlotte. That was a real village inn! I took the public room, which doubled as a dining room, as the subject of my study. The old woman in a headscarf is Mother Antony herself, and that splendid girl serving drinks is her servant Nana. The white poodle is Toto, who had a wooden leg. I had some of my friends, including Sisley and Le Cœur, pose around the table. The motifs that make up the background were borrowed from scenes painted on the wall; they were unpretentious, but often successful paintings by the regulars. I myself drew a sketch of Murger on the wall and copied it in the upper left-hand corner of the painting.'

The earthy realism and sombre muddy colours are strongly reminiscent of the work of the great Realist Gustave Courbet who exercised a great influence on Renoir in the 1860s. For all the picture's youthful charm, it is not entirely surprising that the dark colour did not altogether find favour with the elderly Renoir, who sought, above all, warmth and luminosity in his work.

Portrait of Bazille, 1867

Frédéric Bazille was born in 1841, the same year as Renoir, but came from a very different background. Bazille's family was wealthy, distinguished and cultured. He was originally intended for the medical profession, enrolling in the medical faculty in Montpellier. In 1862 he moved to Paris intending to combine medical studies with artistic studies in the studio of Gleyre where he met Renoir and Monet. Bazille was the first member of the future Impressionist circle to introduce himself to the young Renoir. Renoir was initially surprised that this elegant young man, 'the sort who gives the impression of having his valet break in his new shoes for him', should have approached him, but Bazille explained, 'From the way you draw, I feel that you really are somebody.' Until his tragic death in the Franco-Prussian war of 1870, Bazille was to prove a loyal and generous friend, introducing Renoir to a more sophisticated circle, to the latest ideas of the artistic avant-garde and easing his financial distress with frequent loans and by sharing his studio. At the time this picture was painted Renoir and Monet were sharing Bazille's studio in the rue Visconti. He wrote to his sister, 'Monet has fallen upon me from the skies. Counting Renoir, that makes two hardworking painters I'm housing. I'm delighted.' At the same time that Renoir painted this touching momento of their friendship, Bazille painted an equally casual and intimate portrait of Renoir which remained in Renoir's possession for the rest of his life.

Renoir has shown Bazille hard at work on a still life of dead birds. The picture still exists, as does a version of the same subject by Sisley. While working on this still life and posing for Renoir's portrait, Bazille set aside elegance in favour of practical working clothes and comfortable slippers. Bazille's extreme height, which is so striking in portraits by Manet and Monet, is here somewhat disguised by the pose. The fine brush that Bazille uses is indicative of a technique that was somewhat less broad than that of his collegues.

The painting originally belonged to Manet whose influence it betrays in the cool, 'blonde' tonality, and in the relationship between the sitter and a background that was unusually complex for Renoir. Manet lent the picture to the Second Impressionist Exhibition in 1876, where it was seen by Bazille's father who was so moved by it that he begged to buy it. Manet agreed to swap it for Monet's *Women in the Garden*. The portraits of Bazille by Renoir and of Renoir by Bazille are now reunited in the Musée d'Orsay.

The model for this picture was Renoir's mistress Lise Tréhot. She had met the artist two years earlier in the summer of 1865 when she was 17 years old. Her sister Clémence was already the mistress of Renoir's close friend Jules Le Cœur, and it was no doubt Le Cœur who introduced Lise and Renoir. Lise became Renoir's most frequent model throughout the seven years of their relationship, posing for such important pictures as *The Bather with Griffon, Diana (the Huntress)*, and *The Woman of Algiers*.

The woman with a parasol was the first major picture by Renoir in which he attempted to record the effect of sunlight on the human figure and to analyse the colour of shadows. The picture was a daring one for its date and received mixed reviews when exhibited at the Salon in 1868. The enlightened Thoré-Bürger wrote, 'The dress of white gauze, enriched at the waist by a black ribbon whose ends reach to the ground, is in full light, but with a slight greenish cast from the reflections of the foliage. The head and neck are held in a delicate half-shadow under the shade of a parasol. The effect is so natural and so true that one might very well find it false, because one is accustomed to nature represented in conventional colours.' A less sympathetic critic described the picture unflatteringly as 'a fat woman splashed in white' and accused Renoir of imitating Manet.

Diana (the Huntress), 1867

The more progressive French painters in the 1860s largely shunned mythological subjects, leaving them to the academic masters such as Bouguereau and Cabanel, whose *Birth of Venus* had been the most admired exhibit in the official Salon of 1863. No doubt Renoir hoped to curry favour with the Salon jury by giving his picture such a traditional title. Not surprisingly, the jury was not taken in and the picture was rejected. Renoir's *Diana* has none of the lascivious sexiness of mid nineteenth-century Salon goddesses. This 'goddess' is evidently the artist's plump mistress Lise Tréhot posed in the studio with a dead deer. The deer is not only the attribute of Diana but also a kind of homage to Courbet for whom the dead deer was almost a trademark. The solidly realistic treatment of Lise's body, the application of paint with a palette knife and the predominance of earth colours, confirm Renoir's interest in Courbet at this point. The influence of Courbet was to remain visible in Renoir's art for another three or four years, but it was to be several decades before he painted another picture with a mythological title.

Alfred Sisley was the son of a wealthy English silk merchant, and while his artistic allegiances were thoroughly French, he retained his English nationality. Sisley met Renoir, Bazille and Monet at Gleyre's studio. Though he participated in only four of the eight Impressionist group shows, he was, after Monet, the most completely Impressionist member of the group. Unlike Renoir, he was almost exclusively interested in landscape and remained faithful to Impressionist aims to the end of his life, though he painted with decreasing strength and conviction after 1880.

At the end of his life, Renoir remembered with affection Sisley's gentleness and charm and also his gallantry and flirtatiousness towards women, which is so nicely characterized by his solicitous stance in this picture. Renoir told his son that Sisley 'could never resist a petticoat. We would be walking along the street, talking about the weather or something equally trivial and suddenly Sisley would disappear. Then I would discover him at his old game of flirting.' Sisley's companion in the portrait has traditionally been identified as his wife Eugénie. But a contemporary letter from Renoir to Bazille as well as the physical resemblance and other portraits by Renoir, suggest that the model was in fact Renoir's own mistress Lise Tréhot.

With its sharp tonal contrasts, relatively flattened forms and striking use of black, the painting marks the highpoint of Manet's influence upon Renoir's art.

La Grenouillère, 1869

The series of small riverscapes that Renoir and Monet painted at La Grenouillère in the summer of 1869 can be regarded as the first fully Impressionist pictures. Both artists had intended to paint large, 'finished' versions of the subject to be sent to the Salon. That their ambitions were never realized was probably due to lack of money to pay for the models, quantities of paint and large canvases required for such a project. Eventually they both came to realize that their sparkling sketches had a freshness and directness which could not be reproduced in the studio. For the next decade, painting small-scale landscapes rapidly, on the spot before the motif, became the usual Impressionist practice, and the traditional distinction between sketch and 'finished' work disappeared. During the summer of 1869, Renoir and Monet would set up their easels side by side and paint almost identical subjects and compositions which can only be told apart by their distinctive versions of the broken Impressionist brushwork.

Flowers in a Vase, c. 1869

This undated flower piece was probably painted in 1869, around the time that Renoir and Monet painted the first fully Impressionist landscapes at La Grenouillère. Indeed this painting provides further evidence of the close collaboration of the two artists at this time, as Monet painted a picture of the same vase of flowers, no doubt working once again at Renoir's side. It was to be some years before Renoir's still lifes, interiors and figure painting would catch up with the freedom and luminosity of the landscapes painted out of doors. In this picture, only the looser, less precise application of paint indicates Renoir's progress towards Impressionism. The dark background and relatively muted colours are reminiscent of earlier still lifes, such as the flower piece in the Hamburg Kunsthalle, and of flower pieces painted in the 1860s by Courbet and Fantin-Latour.

Odalisque or Woman of Algiers, 1870

Odalisque belongs to a tradition of Orientalist subjects and fantasies of harem life that goes back to Ingres and Delacroix. The title of the picture openly declares its descent from Delacroix's *Women of Algiers* of 1834. The rich colour, scintillating brushwork, languid eroticism and slightly claustrophobic atmosphere of Delacroix's masterpiece are all reproduced in Renoir's picture. Renoir retained his admiration for Delacroix's *Women of Algiers* to the end of his life. In 1897 when he visited the Louvre with Julie Manet, the young daughter of Berthe Morisot, he paused for a long time in front of Delacroix's picture before saying, 'When you've done something like that you can sleep peacefully at night.'

Renoir was to produce two more paintings obviously indebted to Delacroix: *Parisian Women in Algerian Dress* of 1872 and the *Girl with a Falcon* of 1880, as well as a remarkably faithful copy of Delacroix's *Jewish Wedding* in 1875. It was no doubt largely his admiration for Delacroix which prompted Renoir to go to Algiers himself in 1881.

The Bather with Griffon, 1870

Renoir was fortunate in having two major works accepted by the Salon of 1870, *Odalisque* and *The Bather with Griffon*. The same model (Lise Tréhot) was used for both pictures, but they could hardly be more different: whereas the *Odalisque* is inspired by the colourful Orientalism of Delacroix, the *Bather with Griffon* is heavily indebted to the earthly realism of Courbet. Although this is ostensibly an open-air picture, the colours are far more sombre than those of the *Odalisque* in her harem interior.

The lessons of La Grenouillère have been entirely ignored. The dark earth tones here seem to be a throw back to an earlier stage of Renoir's development, but the solidly sculptural treatment also looks forward to the time when Renoir would react against the formlessness of Impressionism.

The Pont Neuf, 1872

Perhaps influenced by the balloonist-photographer Nadar, both Renoir and Monet painted several views of central Paris with high view points and the summary treatment of moving figures in the 1870s. Their fellow Impressionist Camille Pissarro turned to similar themes and compositions in the 1890s when both Renoir and Monet had long given up Parisian scenes.

Renoir presents us here with one of the more famous views of Paris towards the Île de la Cité and the Latin Quarter on the other side of the river Seine. The equestrian statue of Henry of Navarre and the old buildings on the Île de la Cité are still largely unchanged, though the popular bathing establishment depicted in the bottom right corner of the picture has long disappeared. Renoir's brother Edouard has described how he stopped passers-by on the bridge to ask the time in order to allow Renoir to make rapid sketches from life.

Riding in the Bois de Boulogne, 1873

This strange picture was probably the largest that Renoir ever painted; and is certainly his only equestrian portrait. Renoir's submission to the Salon of 1872 had been rejected, and it seems that the elegant subject matter and ambitious scale of the picture were intended to impress the Salon jury of 1873. Once again though, his efforts were to no avail and the picture was rejected. It can have been small consolation that *Riding in the Bois de Boulogne* was included in an exhibition of rejected pictures organized in emulation of the notorious Salon des Refusés of 1863. Although Renoir had little time for revolutionary gestures, the attitude of the Salon juries of 1872 and 1873 convinced him of the need to take part in the First Impressionist Exhibition in 1874.

When Renoir met Monet in the studio of Gleyre in the early 1860s, it was the beginning of a friendship which was to last until Renoir's death more than a half a century later. The friendship between the two artists was reinforced in the early years by shared hardships and the hostility of the world. It is more surprising that their relationship survived in the years after 1882 when the two artists developed in radically different directions.

In 1882 Monet only agreed to exhibit in the Seventh Impressionist Exhibition if Renoir would do so as well. As late as 1900 when Renoir agreed to accept the order of the Chevalier de la Legion d'Honneur, he still sought the approval of Monet, writing to him, 'I have let them give me a decoration . . . whether or not I have done something stupid, your friendship still means a lot to me.'

Around 1873–4 Monet and Renoir were at their closest artistically. They worked side by side at Monet's home in Argenteuil, painting pictures which look even more alike than the ones they had painted together at La Grenouillère in the summer of 1869 when they created Impressionism.

No doubt Monet was the stronger and more influential of the two artists at this stage, but Renoir had much to offer Monet as well and close scrutiny of even the pictures most similar to those of Monet, reveals evidence of Renoir's individual personality. Like Monet, Renoir builds up a dense and complex paint surface, composed of countless tiny broken touches of paint. But Renoir's brushstrokes are lighter and more delicate than those of Monet and he inclines to a slightly warmer range of colours.

The Gust of Wind, c. 1873

The Gust of Wind is so delightfully evocative of a summer's day spent away from the noise and stress of a big city, that it is hard to understand why such pictures received so hostile a response from the Parisians of the 1870s. One problem was that the viewers of the 1870s felt cheated by the lack of finish. They expected to be able to approach to within a few inches of the picture surface and 'read' every detail. They were also disconcerted by the daringly unconventional approach of the Impressionists to composition and the rendering of space.

In *The Gust of Wind* Renoir does allow, at least in vestigial form, the traditional device of trees used to frame the ends of the composition, but he does not lead the eye back step by step into the distance, as would have the great classical landscapists Claude and Poussin and their academic imitators in the nineteenth century. Conservative art lovers of the 1870s would have seen the grass in the foreground as incoherently applied patches of green paint on the surface of the picture.

Mme. Claude Monet with her Son, 1874

After the Franco-Prussian War Monet and his wife Camille settled at Argenteuil, on the river Seine, within easy reach of central Paris. They were visited there by Renoir, Manet and Sisley and for a while in the mid 1870s Argenteuil became the focal point of the Impressionist movement.

Many years later Monet told a strange and amusing story of how this picture came to be painted: 'This delightful painting by Renoir, which I am so pleased to own, is a portrait of my first wife. It was painted in our garden at Argenteuil when Manet, enchanted by the colour and the light had decided to do an open-air painting of people underneath the trees. While he was working, Renoir arrived. The charm of this hour appealed to him and he asked me for a palette, a brush and a canvas and there he was painting side by side with Manet. Manet watched him out of the corner of his eye and went over to look at his canvas from time to time. He would grimace, step over to me, point at Renoir and whisper in my ear, "That boy has no talent . . . you're his friend, tell him to give up painting!". It was probably no more than a momentary fit of competitive pique that prompted these uncharitable remarks from Manet, though it seems that he appreciated Renoir's Impressionist work less than the style of his portrait of Bazille which Manet had owned and admired for several years.

The long-suffering Camille posed for numerous pictures by Monet and Renoir, indoors and outdoors, in sunshine and snow. Although the resulting paintings have great charm, she is rarely individualized, and it is hard to see her as a personality in her own right, rather than a convenient pictorial prop. Monet painted her for the last time on her deathbed in 1879, observing and analysing the coloured shadows on her face, as though they were effects of sunshine or snow in a landscape.

Renoir's portrait of 1874 is more sketchy and spontaneous than the one Manet painted beside him. The boldly flattened space is reminiscent of a Japanese woodcut print, though as Renoir was generally unenthusiastic about Japanese art, the 'Japanese' effects of his Impressionist phase, may have come to him second-hand via the art of Monet.

La Loge, 1874

Even at the height of the Impressionist movement in the mid 1870s Renoir was never as exclusively committed to open-air painting as his colleagues, Monet, Pissarro and Sisley. In *La Loge*, which was exhibited in the First Impressionist Exhibition of 1874, Renoir tackles the kind of urban night-life subject favoured by Manet and Degas. A painting of a theatre box inevitably invites comparison with Degas, but Renoir's approach to the subject is very different. He ignores the exciting visual possibilities offered by a gas-lit theatre which would have been seized upon by Degas – unusual viewpoints, complex and startling composition and mysterious effects of artificial light. Always more attracted to feminine charm, Renoir concentrates instead on the worldly elegance of the woman occupying the box. She regards us with the calm and slightly vacant expression with which Renoir so often graces his female sitters. She was described by one contemporary artist as 'one of those women with pearly white cheeks and the light of some banal passion in their eyes . . . attractive, worthless, delicious and stupid'. Despite hostile reactions to the exhibition as a whole, *La Loge* was singled out for praise by several critics.

La Loge challenges the widely held belief that the Impressionists banished black from their palettes. The blacks of the lady's striped dress and the gentleman's jacket set off magnificently the roses and pearls of her dress and of her complexion.

Self-Portrait, 1875

Renoir portraits rarely attempt to go beyond the surface to reveal much of the sitter's personality. However beautifully painted, most of his portraits are psychologically bland. This self-portrait is exceptional in capturing something of the nervosity which many friends observed in the young Renoir. The tense expression is no doubt partly due to the effort of concentration as he observes himself in the mirror. The year of this portrait was a difficult one for Renoir. Following the financial and critical failure of the First Impressionist Exhibition, Renoir organized an auction of Impressionist paintings at the Hotel Drouot with even more disastrous consequences. The twenty paintings which Renoir sent to this auction were sold at depressingly low prices. To add to his misery, he was rejected once again at the Salon. None of these misfortunes affected the *joie-de-vivre* of the sunlit landscapes and charming female portraits which Renoir painted in 1875.

Portrait of M. Chocquet, 1876

It was the disastrous sale of Impressionist pictures organized by Renoir at the Hotel Drouot in 1875 that brought the remarkable Victor Chocquet into the artist's life. Despite the abuse shouted by angry members of the public and the conditions of near riot, Chocquet was deeply impressed by the Impressionist pictures, and in particular by those of Renoir. The evening after the sale Chocquet wrote to Renoir asking if he would be willing to paint a portrait of his wife. On the modest salary of a customs official Chocquet built up a magnificent collection that included superb eighteenth-century French furniture and paintings by Watteau, Delacroix and Courbet. To these were soon added masterpieces by Renoir, Monet and Cézanne. Renoir called Chocquet 'the greatest French art collector since the days of the kings or perhaps of the whole world since the Popes'. Chocquet became a passionate advocate of Impressionism when few people could understand it. According to Degas' friend Théodore Duret, Chocquet harangued hostile visitors to the Second Impressionist Exhibition 'in order to persuade them of his convictions, to make them share his admiration and pleasure. It was a thankless task, but Chocquet was not to be disheartened.' Chocquet's faith in Renoir was to be rewarded by two of the finest male portraits that Renoir ever painted. Both show a degree of psychological penetration which is very rare in Renoir's portraiture, and which must have resulted from the warm friendship and understanding between the two men. In this one Renoir conveys a relaxed mood and good-humoured charm. The pose with clasped hands was obviously a characteristic one, since Chocquet also adopts it in a well-known portrait of him by Cézanne. He is shown against one of his several paintings by Delacroix, an artist whom he revered and with whom he liked to compare Renoir. Chocquet had already requested that Renoir should paint his wife against the background of a Delacroix, explaining, 'I want to have you together, you and Delacroix.'

Nude in the Sunlight, 1876

Renoir painted far fewer nudes in the 1870s than in any other decade of his career. The reason for this was most probably his preoccupation during the Impressionist period with painting in the open air. It was difficult enough to paint a landscape outside the controlled environment of the studio without the added problems of posing a nude model.

Nude in the Sunlight was shown at the Second Impressionist Exhibition of 1876 under the title of *Study No 212* (yet another example of the Impressionist indifference to poetic titles). It excited a good deal of hostile comment because of its lack of finish, the unidealized treatment of the nude and above all for the way in which Renoir depicted the play of dappled light on the model's skin.

The effect of sunlight breaking through foliage was one that fascinated Renoir in the 1870s. It was an effect that artists had rarely attempted to capture before, and particularly not on the human figure. Nineteenth-century viewers failed to understand what the artist was trying to do. Albert Wolff, the fiercely reactionary art critic of *Le Figaro*, described the nude as a 'Mass of flesh in the process of decomposition with green and violet spots which denote the state of complete putrefaction of a corpse!'

Renoir had to endure such comments through much of his career. As late as the 1890s the German author Max Nordau wrote of a painting by Renoir of a woman 'on whose skin light and shadows play so unfortunately that she looks as if studded with corpse-stains of putrescence in the second degree'.

The Swing, 1876

Renoir was almost certainly aware of the paintings by Fragonard, Hubert Robert and other eighteenth-century French painters of swings. His passion for eighteenth-century French masters went back to the time when he copied the works of Watteau and Boucher on to porcelain plates as a young boy. Many of Renoir's paintings in the 1870s have the idyllic and *galant* mood of a Watteau *Fête champêtre* or a Boucher *Pastorale*. It was as though Renoir wished to translate the masters into a modern idiom. His friend Georges Rivière noted the connection when he reviewed the Third Impressionist Exhibition in which it was shown, remarking, 'We have to go back to Watteau to find a painting with the charm that pervades *The Swing*.' The modernity of the picture lay not only in the fashionable clothes of the models but more particularly in the striking way that Renoir rendered the broken patches of sunlight on the girl's dress. This was a disturbing feature for many contemporary critics, including G. Vassy of *L'Evénement* who wrote, 'the sunlight effects are combined in such a bizarre fashion that they look like spots of grease on the model's clothes.'

Renoir worked simultaneously on *The Swing* and the *Moulin de la Galette*, painting *The Swing* in the overgrown garden of his studio in the rue Cortot in the mornings and moving on to the *Moulin de la Galette* in the afternoons.

Moulin de la Galette, 1876

Moulin de la Galette was the largest and most ambitious picture that Renoir painted in the 1870s while his Impressionist phase was at its height. As a rule the Impressionists' insistence during this decade on painting out of doors restricted them to small canvases and relatively simple composition. It would have represented a considerable *tour de force* to paint such a large picture out of doors, braving changes of light and weather conditions and gusts of wind that threatened to send canvas and artist flying. We have the word of Renoir's friend Georges Rivière that the artist did indeed carry the canvas every day to the Moulin de la Galette from his nearby studio in the rue Cortot.

The Moulin de la Galette was an open air dance-hall on the Butte Montmartre above central Paris, where young artists and students could meet *grisettes*, young girls out for a good time, and willing often enough to pose for or to sleep with an impoverished artist. Renoir gives us a charming and no doubt, rosy picture of 'la vie de Bohème' in nineteenth-century Montmartre. A few decades later Toulouse-Lautrec and the young Picasso would offer a much harsher view of the same milieu, but Renoir chose to ignore poverty, disease, ugliness and anything the least bit sordid. Instead he gives us one of the most glorious celebrations of youthful *joie-de-vivre* in the history of Western art. The young men were identified by Rivière as Renoir's friends Lestringuez, a civil servant, the journalist Lhote and the artists Franc-Lamy, Goeneutte, Cordey and Gervex. Strangely none of these artists belonged to the Impressionist group. Gervex became immensely rich and successful by painting slightly scandalous subjects in a technique which combined the fresh colour and open-air effects of the Impressionists with a slick academic drawing.

Moulin de la Galette was bought by the artist collector Gustave Caillebotte. The picture's large size, 'vulgar' subject matter and daring effects of broken sunlight would have made it hard to sell and Caillebotte probably bought it largely to help out the impoverished Renoir.

The First Outing, 1876

The title *The First Outing* was not given to this picture by Renoir, but it is easy to see why the painting lent itself to such an anecdotal interpretation. It exhibits a prettiness that hovers on the brink of sentimentality. Renoir was never ashamed of prettiness. Toward the end of his life he wrote, 'For me a picture must be lovable, cheerful and pretty, yes pretty ... There are enough tiresome things in life already without our taking the trouble to produce more.' Renoir painted a number of pictures of theatre interiors in the mid 1870s which invite comparison with Degas. Of these pictures, *The First Outing* comes closest to Degas's highly idiosyncratic compositional methods with the juxtaposition of near and far. Renoir does not contrast the lighting of the theatre box with the scene below as Degas might have done, but he does convey the animation of the crowd by means of loose, broken brushwork.

Garden in the rue Cortot, Montmartre, 1876

When Renoir moved to Montmartre in the 1870s, it was already at the height of its reputation as a centre of 'La vie de Bohème'. Though it was encircled by urban and industrial developments and the foundations of the great Basilica of the Sacre-Coeur were in the process of being laid at the summit of the hill, Montmartre still retained a semi-rural air. According to his friend Georges Rivière, Renoir chose to live in the rue Cortot because of its proximity to the Moulin de la Galette which he wished to paint and because he found a lodging with a beautiful garden. 'As soon as Renoir crossed the threshold,' Rivière recalled, 'he was delighted with the sight of the garden, which looked like a beautiful neglected park. Passing through the narrow hall of the little house, one found oneself facing a huge lawn of unmown grass dotted with poppies, convolvulus and daisies. Beyond that, a fine avenue of mature trees and beyond that again an orchard and vegetable garden, then a shrubbery . . . ' Renoir's magical painting evokes a luxuriant and rather mysterious secret garden. The tall format (unusual for a landscape) and the lack of any visible sky increase its strange and hermetic effect.

The Woman with Umbrella and Child, c. 1874–1876.

The Woman with Umbrella and Child is a small, loosely brushed work which has all the hall-marks of having been rapidly executed in the open air. The lack of a horizon and of any of the traditional props and devices for conveying recession creates a spacial ambiguity which is typical of many of Renoir's landscapes in the 1870s. It is a feature which Renoir shared with Monet, but the tenderness with which the mother and child are depicted and the fluffy delicate brushwork are unmistakably characteristic of Renoir.

Mme. Charpentier and her Children, 1878

Renoir's meeting with the publisher Georges Charpentier and his wife marked a turning point in his career. In the famous literary and political salon of Mme. Charpentier, he moved for the first time in fashionable society and his portrait of *Mme. Charpentier and her Children* exhibits a new found sophistication. Thanks to the powerful influence of the Charpentiers, the picture was favourably hung at the Salon and on the whole enthusiastically received by the critics who praised the charming informality of the composition and Renoir's dazzling skill as a colourist.

Critical voices were raised, however. One dismissed the portrait as 'a slack, transparent sketch, which seems to have been done with different coloured balls of cotton wool . . . ' It was a description which might have been understandable if applied to one of Renoir's late paintings, but the fact that it was used for one of the most densely and carefully finished works he ever painted demonstrated just how conservative critical taste could be in the late 1870s. At the age of 37, after many years of hardship and rejection Renoir was desperate to win success and acceptance as an artist. With this portrait he clearly pulled out every stop in order to please. The densely worked, shimmering paint surface is a breathtaking *tour de force*. The almost over-rich decorative effect created by the use of oriental props anticipates the kind of *Belle Epoque* society portraiture practised by John Singer Sargent and his imitators in the following decades.

The rewards of fashionable portraiture were huge. The popular but extremely dull portraitist Laure-Lévy Bonnat could command thirty times the already generous fee that Renoir received for the portrait of Mme. Charpentier and her children. Thanks to the contacts he made at the salon of Mme. Charpentier, it seemed for a short time in the late 1870s and early 1880s that Renoir too could embark upon the career of a fashionable portraitist, but he was deflected from this course by the stylistic experiments of his 'dry' period.

This portrait is exceptional in Renoir's œuvre in its use of Far-Eastern props. According to Renoir's brother Edouard, Renoir did not carefully choose all the objects in the picture, as aesthetes such as Manet, Whistler and Sargent would have done. He merely painted Mme. Charpentier's home as it was. Renoir did not share the enthusiasm of so many of his contemporaries for 'all that one sees that is Japanese'.

The Skiff, c. 1879

A sunny day, pleasure boats on the river Seine, reflections in water, a suburban villa, a slice of a railway bridge, a train rushing past, emphasizing the transience of the scene, all these elements add up to an archetypal Impressionist picture of the kind that Monet painted countless times in the 1870s. Renoir's picture with its broken brushwork and its daringly open composition with no framing motifs is certainly close to the work of his fellow Impressionist, but Renoir's hand is easily discernible in the light and feathery version of the Impressionist brush-stroke. The brush-stroke varies throughout the picture, short, horizontal, comma-like strokes for the shimmering surface of the water, vertical or diagonal strokes for the foliage in the foreground and more dense and solid application of paint for the orange boat, and the brightly lit walls in the background.

This sparkling picture once belonged to the collector Victor Chocquet, who, as a great admirer of Delacroix, would certainly have appreciated Renoir's bold juxtaposition of the complementary blue and orange.

Portrait of Mlle. Irène Cahen d'Anvers, 1880

Following the great success of his Portrait of *Mme. Charpentier and her Children*, Renoir was in great demand for portraits of children, of which he produced a great many in the years around 1880. Among the finest were the portraits of her daughters commissioned by Mme. Cahen d'Anvers, the wife of a wealthy Jewish banker. Renoir obviously responded to the delicate beauty of the eldest daughter Irène. In particular he seems to have enjoyed painting the wealth of golden hair cascading over her shoulders. Unusually among his commissioned portraits Irène Cahen d'Anvers does not look out at the viewer but seems lost in her own rather sad thoughts. The expression of melancholy may have been induced by boredom. The sittings were presumably long ones, as only two were required for what is a relatively highly finished portrait. The equally delightful portrait of the younger daughters Elizabeth and Alice was not liked by the Cahen d'Anvers family who relegated it to the servants quarters. Mme Cahen d'Anvers preferred to have her own portrait done by the fashionable but far more expensive artist Laure-Lèvy Bonnat, so missing the opportunity to share in her daughters' immortality. The slowness of the Cahen d'Anvers in paying Renoir occasioned an outburst of the anti-Semitism which was never far from the surface with Renoir. However, he remained on friendly terms with M. Cahen d'Anvers' younger brother Albert, of whom he also painted a fine portrait.

The Luncheon of the Boating Party, 1880–1881

The Luncheon of the Boating Party was largely painted in the summer of 1880, a year before Renoir's trip to Italy and his subsequent move away from Impressionism. Although the painting may be regarded as the crowning achievement of Renoir's Impressionist phase, signs of impending change are already visible. The awning under which the figures sit creates a more even light than Renoir had painted in such pictures of the mid 1870s as *Moulin de la Galette* and *The Swing*. Shimmering light and atmosphere bathe the superbly painted still life on the table, but the light no longer threatens to dissolve the integrity of the figures. Contours are firmer and the composition is more clearly structured.

This picture is the first document of Renoir's love for his future wife Aline Charigot. According to early sources she posed for the charming young girl in the bottom left corner, playing with a small dog. At this date she was no more than pleasingly plump and with her full, wide mouth and short, turn-up nose she corresponded perfectly to Renoir's ideal of feminine beauty. Although the faces are more defined than those of the figures in *Moulin de la Galette*, they are not strongly characterized, and all the young girls have a strong family resemblance to one another as was so often the case in Renoir's paintings.

The young man in a straw hat sitting opposite Aline Charigot was posed for by Gustave Caillebotte, the generous friend and patron of the Impressionists. Caillebotte was an enthusiastic oarsman and also a gifted painter who exhibited in several of the Impressionist shows. In the late 1870s he anticipated Renoir by painting several pictures of boating parties, but it is hard to imagine Renoir wishing to paint the strenuous activities of the oarsmen on the river as Caillebotte had done. Instead Renoir chooses to paint a moment of relaxation and flirtation. The opportunity to meet young girls was one of the chief attractions of such boating expeditions as has been recorded by another keen oarsmen, the writer Guy de Maupassant. The painting may be regarded as a translation into everyday nineteenth-century reality, of the kind of 'Fête champètre' painted by Watteau 150 years earlier.

It is appropriate that the culminating masterpiece of Renoir's Impressionist phase should have been painted beside the river Seine at a short distance from La Grenouillère where the movement had been born eleven years before.

Blonde Bather, 1881

Blonde Bather records the already ample figure of the young Aline Charigot, Renoir's future wife, who accompanied him on his trip to Italy in 1881. Renoir claimed to have painted the picture in the open air in a boat in the Bay of Naples. If this was so, the contrast between the *Blonde Bather* and the *Nude in the Sunlight* painted five years earlier becomes all the more telling. Renoir no longer seeks to capture ephemeral effects of light and atmosphere and to fuse the figure with her surroundings.

Impressed by the Pompeian wall paintings he had seen in Naples and the Raphael frescos he had seen in Rome, Renoir now attempted a timeless, idealized and monumental treatment of the female nude. The *Blonde Bather* marked a turning point in the artist's development and proved to be the prototype for his innumerable later depictions of the female nude.

Arab Festival, 1881

In 1881 Renoir was able to travel to North Africa in the knowledge that the support of the dealer Paul Durand-Ruel had bought him a measure of financial security for the first time. The two lengthy journeys that Renoir made in the course of that year were also a sign of the restlessness that was to lead him away from Impressionism. Like many nineteenth-century French painters Renoir had already essayed Orientalist fantasies, but as in the case of Delacroix half a century earlier Renoir was deeply impressed by the reality of the Arab world and excited by the intensity of light in North Africa and by the nobility and grace of its inhabitants. He told his son Jean, 'In Algeria I discovered white. Everything is white, the walls, the minaret, the road.' Whites certainly play an important role in these pictures. Renoir employs the full panoply of Impressionist technique to convey the shimmering heat haze, the animation of the crowd and the frenzied movements of the dancers. Individual figures are dissolved in light and atmosphere, but Renoir combines a dazzling Impressionist paint surface with a more carefully structured composition.

Renoir told Ambroise Vollard that when he delivered the picture to Durand-Ruel, 'it looked like a heap of crumbled plaster. Durand-Ruel trusted me, and several years later the colour had done its work, and the subject emerged from the canvas as I had concieved it.' In 1900 Claude Monet bought the picture from Durand-Ruel. It is not surprising that the author of the Rouan Cathedral series should have admired the luminosity and dense technique of this picture.

Still Life with Onions, 1881

This tiny painting of onions shows that Renoir, like Chardin a hundred years earlier, was capable of producing great art from the humblest and most insignificant subject matter and on the smallest scale. The charm of the picture lies in its apparent informality. The onions and garlic appear to have been cast down haphazardly. In fact each element is locked into a complex and carefully premeditated composition in which no element could be moved without disturbing the harmony of the whole. The bordered cloth and the onions form a lop-sided triangle, with the long diagonal on the left created by the blue and red border and the isolated onion answered by steeper diagonals on the right, culminating in the onion at the apex of the group. The composition is further united by the elliptical far side of the table top. The liveliness of Renoir's touch and the bulging shapes of the onions pointing in different directions give the little painting a Baroque exuberance.

The Umbrellas, c. 1881–1885

Despite or because of his instinctive and non-intellectual approach to his art, Renoir changed his style more often and more radically than any of the other Impressionists. *The Umbrellas* offers striking visual evidence of what was perhaps the most important change in direction of Renoir's art. On grounds of style and also of the fashions worn by the women in the picture, it is assumed that *The Umbrellas* was begun around 1881 and finished about four years later. The modern life subject-matter suggests Renoir's Impressionist phase, as does the broken, feathery brushwork with which the figures on the right are painted. The girl on the left carrying a hat box shows a very different technique, with sharply defined contours, smooth, unbroken flesh tones and smaller regular brush-strokes in the almost sculpturally modelled dress. Despite the stylistic discrepancies the picture has become one of Renoir's most popular since it entered the London National Gallery in 1917 as part of the Hugh Lane Bequest. Unlike Monet, Pissarro or Sisley, Renoir very rarely painted bad or wintry weather. He disliked the cold and thought that snow was 'one of Nature's illnesses'. He was probably persuaded to paint a rainy day by the charmingly decorative effect created by the repeated shapes of the umbrellas. It was an effect popular among Japanese woodcut artists and taken up by many European painters in the late nineteenth century.

Portrait of Charles and Georges Durand-Ruel, 1882

Double or group portraits frequently stimulated Renoir to more inventive composition and more interesting poses with which to characterize the sitters. In this double portrait Renoir successfully conveys the relaxed and informal relationship of the two young brothers, sons of his dealer Paul Durand-Ruel.

Paul Durand-Ruel began to buy Renoir's work in the early 1870s when no other dealer was interested and became the chief source of Renoir's income from 1881, when he began to buy Renoir's work in quantity. Although Renoir later sold pictures to Vollard and Bernheim Jeune, he continued to do business with Durand-Ruel and never forgot the help the dealer had given him. Durand-Ruel's sons were regarded by Renoir almost as members of his family and Georges was invited by Mme. Renoir to be godfather of her son Jean.

The portrait of Charles and Georges Durand-Ruel belongs to a series which their father commissioned in 1882 of all five of his children. The situation of the portrait in the open air against a background of foliage would seem to offer opportunities of painting those effects of dappled light which had so delighted Renoir in the 1870s, but by 1882 Renoir was already leaving Impressionism behind him. Effects of light and atmosphere are kept firmly under control and the Impressionist weave of broken colour is confined within well-defined contours.

Dance at Bougival, 1882–1883

Dance at Bougival is one of a series of three near life-size pictures of dancing couples painted between 1882 and 1883. The subject matter, a celebration of the simple everyday pleasures of modern urban or suburban life, belongs to Renoir's Impressionist phase. They were the last major treatment of such modern life themes apart from *The Umbrellas*, begun earlier but finished later. The firm contours and clarity of composition show that Renoir was already leaving Impressionism behind him. *Dance at Bougival* could almost be an illustration for a novel or short story by Guy de Maupassant, and Renoir did in fact use a drawing based on the composition to illustrate a short story by his friend Paul Lhote, published in the newspaper *La Vie Moderne* in 1883. The model for the girl was apparently Suzanne Valadon, later to become a distinguished artist herself, though her gaunt and strong features are hardly recognizable in Renoir's plump and pretty dancer.

Portrait of Paul Haviland, 1884

Renoir adopts a formal pose for this touching but entirely unsentimental portrait of a little boy in a sailor suit. Paul Haviland's pale, transparent complexion stands out from a background which for Renoir is unusually dark. A year or so earlier Renoir had written jokingly to his friend and patron Paul Bernard, 'I'm delighted by what's happening to me now. I'm going to return to the true path and I'm going to enter the studio of Bonnat. In a year or two I'll be able to earn 300,000,000,000,000 francs a year. Don't talk to me any more about portraits in sunlight. A nice dark background, that's the right thing.'

The Children's Afternoon at Wargemont, 1884

Children's Afternoon at Wargemont shows the three daughters of Renoir's friend Paul Berard: the fourteen-year-old Marthe absorbed in her sewing on the right, the four-year-old Lucie holding a doll and the ten-year-old Marguerite, reading a book on a sofa, on the left. The diplomat and banker Paul Berard was one of a group of wealthy patrons that Renoir met at the fashionable salon of Mme. Charpentier in the late 1870s. Berard soon became a close friend of the artist, commissioning several pictures from him and inviting him to stay at his country home at Wargemont near Dieppe. It was during one of these stays that the picture was painted in the summer of 1884.

Children's Afternoon at Wargemont was painted at the height of Renoir's 'dry' period. It is a curiously austere painting in comparison with the portrait of Mme. Charpentier and her children painted six years earlier. Renoir's preoccupation with the art of the past is very evident in the picture. The severe lineality, chalky, high-keyed colours and the slightly naïve stiffness of the figures are reminiscent of fifteenth-century Italian frescos, whereas the complex pattern of verticals and horizontals shows Renoir's awareness of the seventeenth-century Dutch masters.

La Roche-Guyon, c. 1885

La Roche-Guyon was painted at the height of Renoir's experimental phase in the mid 1880s. As much as *The Children's Afternoon at Wargemont* and the *Large Bathers* this picture shows Renoir's desire to escape from the informality and formlessness of Impressionism. This time, though, Renoir has turned for help not to Ingres and Renaissance frescos, but to Cézanne, who joined Renoir at La Roche-Guyon in the summer of 1885. Cézanne too had the ambition to make something solid of Impressionism and to combine it with 'the art of the museums'. Renoir has adopted Cézanne's method of building up the picture surface by means of short, parallel strokes of paint creating a structured or faceted effect. Renoir was one of the very few people of his day capable of appreciating the more difficult and demanding genius of Cézanne and was instrumental in introducing him to his first important collector Victor Chocquet and to the dealer Ambroise Vollard who was eventually to establish Cézanne's reputation. In turn, Cézanne once said that the only two contemporary painters that he did not despise were Renoir and Monet.

The Large Bathers, 1887

The Large Bathers, which Renoir exhibited at the Galerie Georges Petit in the spring of 1887, marked the culmination of his 'dry' style. He had worked on the picture for three years producing numerous prepatory studies in pencil, ink, chalk or watercolour. This in itself shows the distance he had travelled since the days of Impressionism when he and his collegues attempted to work as spontaneously as possible and rarely made any drawings. In contrast with the *Nude in the Sunlight* of 1875, Renoir no longer tries to integrate the figures with their surroundings by means of dappled sunlight and enveloping atmosphere. Instead he concentrates on conveying the weight and volume of the sharply delineated and smoothly painted figures, which stand out clearly from the background. It is clear that neither the figures nor the background were painted in the open air.

Like Cézanne, Renoir wished at this stage of his career to combine the study of nature with what he could learn from 'the art of the museums'. Raphael and Ingres, artists for whom the other Impressionists had little sympathy, provided Renoir with inspiration, but the direct source of the composition and the subject was a seventeenth-century relief sculpture by François Girardon from the ornamental pond in the Allée des Marmousets in the park at Versailles.

The Large Bathers caused considerable dismay among Renoir's friends and admirers when it was first exhibited. It was perhaps understandable that Paul Durand-Ruel should not have liked the picture since Renoir chose to show it in the gallery of a rival dealer, but Pissarro wrote to his son, 'I do not understand what he is trying to do, it is not proper to want to stand still, but he chooses to concentrate on line, his figures are all separate entities, detached from one another without regard for colour.' One of the few who did understand what Renoir was trying to do was the painter Berthe Morisot. After a visit to Renoir's studio in 1886, she wrote, 'He is a draughtsman of first-rate strength; all his prepatory study for a painting would be curious to show the public who generally imagine that the Impressionists work only in the most free and easy manner. I think that one cannot go further in the rendering of form . . . '

The Large Bathers is undoubtably an impressive work, but strangely artificial and lacking many of the more attractive qualities associated with Renoir's art.

Bather Arranging her Hair, c. *1887–1890*

Visitors to the London National Gallery who have known this picture in reproduction only are always surprised by the tiny dimensions of the canvas (15½ × 11½ ins). Despite the size of the picture, the breadth of Renoir's conception of the seated nude could be described as monumental. This little picture marks Renoir's return to a softer, more sensuous handling of paint after the austerity of his 'dry' period, but it does not show a return to the preoccupations of Impressionism. The picture conveys an impression of air and sunlight, but Renoir continues to be concerned with the volume and weight of the figure; and the contours though not sharply delineated, are certainly firmly implied. The paint surface has taken on that lovely nacreous quality which was to characterize Renoir's work for over nearly three decades.

Young Girls at the Piano, 1892

In 1890 Renoir turned down the offer of a decoration from the French state. Nevertheless, he was sufficiently impressed by the offer of official patronage a year or so later to give immense trouble to the painting of *Young Girls at the Piano*, the first picture by Renoir to be bought by the state. He worked simultaneously on six different versions of the subject, allowing final choice to the Minister of Fine Arts. Renoir later came to feel that he had overworked the picture and that the choice made by the state had been the wrong one. Nevertheless, the painting is a fine achievement and thoroughly characteristic of Renoir's work in the 1890s in its theme of pretty young girls making music and also in its silky surface texture.

Gabrielle with Jean, 1900

The births of Renoir's three sons, Pierre (1885), Jean (1894), and Claude (1901) were nicely spaced so as to provide him with child models over a period of more than twenty-five years. Renoir's affection for his children was expressed in countless paintings. At about the time this picture was executed Renoir wrote, 'One must be personally involved in what one does . . . At the moment I'm painting Jean pouting. It's no easy thing, but it's such a lovely subject, and I assure you that I'm working for myself and myself alone.' The birth of Jean also brought into the Renoir household the young girl who was to become Renoir's most frequent model: a cousin of Mme. Renoir, Gabrielle Renard who was hired as a nursemaid to the new baby. She remained as a member of Renoir's inner family circle for nearly twenty years. Jean Renoir tells many stories of Gabrielle's earthy wit and common sense. She was often given the task of posing with Jean and keeping the baby happy while Renoir painted them both. It seems that posing for their father was not the unpleasant chore for Renoir's children, that posing for Augustus John was for his children. Renoir was happy for his child models to play with toys and chatter. In later years when immobility was required for a particular detail of a painting, Gabrielle would be asked to read from Hans Andersen's *Tales*.

Sleeping Woman, 1897

Sleeping Woman is one of Renoir's most voluptuous nudes. The raised arms suggest sensuous abandon as well as showing off the young girl's breasts to best advantage. We cannot believe for a moment that she is asleep or that she is unaware of being watched and admired despite her closed eyes. Renoir's nudes are pin-ups, not so far removed in conception from the centre-fold of a men's magazine. Yet, however earthy and sensuous, they have an air of innocence and simplicity that separates them from the pretty girls painted by the popular Salon painters of the day, who seem lubricious even when fully clothed. The difference lies above all in the facial expression. Renoir never allows his young girls to ogle or entice the viewer as do those of Cabanel, Bouguereau and Gervex. The year before this picture was painted the writer Gustave Geffroy described Renoir's nudes as 'little instinctive beings, at the same time children and women, to whom Renoir brings a convinced love and a malicious observation. They are a wholly individual idea, these young girls who are sensual without vice, oblivious without cruelty, irresponsible though gently woken into life . . . They exist like children; but also like playful young animals, and like flowers which absorb the air and the dew.'

Portrait of Misia Edwards, 1906

By the early 1900s Renoir was besieged by wealthy society women wishing to be immortalized by the master. Luckily he was in the happy position of being able to pick and choose among them. Those whom he found unpleasing and pretentious were turned away empty-handed. One already wealthy woman who pleased him very much was the subject of this picture, Misia Edwards. During her former marriage to the publisher Thadée Natanson she had been the muse of the group of painters known as the 'Nabis'; she had been frequently painted by Bonnard, Vuillard, Valloton and also by Toulouse-Lautrec.

The almost bovine serenity of this portrait is expressive more of Renoir's feminine ideal than of the true personality of this brilliant woman who dominated Parisian cultural life for over forty years and who provided inspiration for two leading characters in Proust's *Á la Recherche du Temps Perdu*.

Like many other artists and men of genius, the aged Renoir seems to have been somewhat infatuated by Misia. He painted a series of eight portraits of her. In 1906 he wrote her a letter which gives a charming glimpse of his feelings: 'Come, and I promise you that in the seventh portrait I shall try to make you even more beautiful. I am well and I'll feel even better if you can come to see me in Essoyes-Aube this summer. I shall do everything I can to show you amusing things and we'll eat as well as possible.'

In her memoirs, Misia recalled that Renoir had begged her to open her blouse and allow him to paint her breasts: 'Lower, lower I beg you,' he insisted. 'My God! why won't you show your breasts? Its criminal!' 'Several times I saw him on the verge of tears when I refused. No one could appreciate better than he the texture of skin, or, in painting, give it such rare pearl-like transparency. After his death I often reproached myself for not letting him see all he wanted. In retrospect my prudishness seems to me stupid, since it was a question of an artist whose extraordinary eye suffered terribly when he was not allowed to see what he guessed was beautiful.'

Portrait of Ambroise Vollard, 1908

The dealer Ambroise Vollard introduced himself to Renoir in the mid 1890s and played an important role in the last two decades of the artist's career. Vollard understood the essentially sculptural quality of Renoir's late nudes and persuaded the artist that he should take up the medium of sculpture. In 1913 Vollard arranged for a young former assistant of the sculptor Maillol to execute sculptures after Renoir's drawings, under the artist's supervision. Prophetically in this portrait of 1908, Vollard is shown holding a small statuette of Maillol. Aristide Maillol had begun his career in the 1890s painting pictures in the flat decorative style of the Nabis group. Failing eyesight had forced him to abandon painting in favour of sculpture. He became the leader of a generation of sculptors in revolt against the overwhelming influence of Rodin. Maillol was profoundly influenced by the late nudes of Renoir, which with their large simple volumes, he found more 'sculptural' than the theatrically expressive and over-naturalistic bronzes of Rodin. Renoir shared the younger artist's mistrust of Rodin, finding him pretentious and on one occasion dismissing an excessively naturalistic Rodin bust as 'smelling of armpit'.

Renoir and Maillol were brought together at about the time of this portrait by Vollard, who commissioned Maillol to make a portrait bust of Renoir. Jean Renoir wrote amusingly of the mishaps that befell Maillol's bust, but a friendship as well as a mutual admiration was established between the two artists. Renoir seems to have been influenced in turn by the younger artist when he came to make his own sculpture.

The Clown, 1909

Renoir once said, 'I want a red to be sonorous, to sound like a bell.' This portrait is an example of the increasingly hot ranges of colour chosen by Renoir after 1900. The red does indeed sound like a bell against the muted pinks and yellows of the background and the important contrast of black provided by the little boy's cap. The picture was posed for by Renoir's youngest son Claude or 'Coco' who inspired many of his best pictures in the first decade of the century. Though 9 years old when the picture was painted, Coco still has long hair. Renoir insisted on his sons keeping their childish long hair for as long as possible, maintaining that it would protect their heads from blows, but also no doubt because he loved to paint it. Claude Renoir later remembered the discomfort of posing for the picture: 'The costume was completed with white stockings which I obstinately refused to put on. My father demanded the stockings in order to finish the picture, but he could do nothing; they pricked me. So my mother bought some silk stockings; they tickled me. Threats followed and then negotiations; one after the other I was promised a spanking, an electric railway, being sent off to a boarding school, and a box of oil colours. Finally I agreed to put on cotton stockings for a few moments; my father, holding back a rage which was ready to burst out, finished the picture despite the contortions I was making to scratch myself. The railway and the box of colours rewarded so much effort.'

Mme. Renoir with her Dog Bob, 1910

In the nineteenth century it was widely believed that artistic genius and domestic happiness were inimical to one another. In George Bernard Shaw's *Man and Superman*, the character of John Tanner expresses this view, declaring that 'of all of human struggles there is none so treacherous and rewardless as the struggle between the artist man and the other woman. Which shall use up the other? That is the issue between them.' Among the great nineteenth-century painters who remained single, fearing that marriage would interfere with their creativity, were Delacroix, Corot, Courbet, Degas, Moreau and Munch. In the case of Renoir, though, his wife can claim a substantial portion of the credit for his later work. By devoting herself unselfishly to Renoir's comfort and happiness and weaving a protective cocoon around him she enabled him to give his best despite the encroachment of illness. Though only about 50 years old when this portrait was painted, Mme. Renoir was herself in poor health and appears much older. She died five years later, predeceasing Renoir by four years.

The Bathers, c. 1918–1919

The Bathers was Renoir's last major work, and consciously painted as a kind of summing up of his preoccupations over the previous thirty years. As he was by then confined to a wheel-chair he was only able to work on such a large canvas (43½ × 63 ins) by means of an adjustable easel, with the canvas on rollers, which enabled him to reach every part of the picture surface. The picture was painted in a specially constructed garden studio at Les Collettes which combined the benefits of working in the open with some degree of protection from the weather and control over the light.

The model for the lower figure was the lovely redhead Andrée Hessling, who was later to marry Renoir's son Jean. Renoir's pneumatic treatment of the female body makes an obvious parallel with the final masterpiece of another great master of the female nude, the *Turkish Bath* of Ingres. In both cases the women are of a cushion-like, almost vegetal passivity. Their soft, swelling, boneless bodies are disturbingly reminiscent of inflated dolls. Renoir's final masterpiece offends deeply against modern canons of female beauty, not to mention feminist sensibilities. Nevertheless, the image is a powerful one and wherever one cares to look the paint is applied with exciting confidence and fluidity. It is perhaps a sign of the painting's strength that it has maintained its ability to arouse controversy.

SELECTED BIBLIOGRAPHY

ANDRÉ, Albert, *Renoir*, Paris, 1919.
ARTS COUNCIL, *Renoir*, Exhibition Catalogue, London, 1985.
DAULTE, F., *Renoir, catalogue raisonné de l'œuvre peint*, (1860–1890), 1st of 4 volumes, Lausanne, 1971.
DENVIR, Bernard (ed.), *The Impressionists at First Hand*, London, 1987.
MEIER-GRAEFE, J., *Auguste Renoir*, Paris, 1912.
PACH, W., *Renoir*, New York, 1950.
PISSARRO, Camille, *Letters to his Son Lucien*, ed. J. Rewald, London, 1980.
PERRUCHOT, H., *La Vie de Renoir*, Paris, 1962.
RENOIR, Jean, *Renoir*, Paris, 1962.
REWALD, John, *The History of Impressionism*, London, 1973.
RIVIÈRE, Georges, *Renoir et ses amis*, Paris, 1921.
VOLLARD, A., *Auguste Renoir*, Paris, 1920.
——*Souvenirs d'un marchand de tableaux*, Paris, 1937.

PHOTOGRAPH CREDITS

CHRONOLOGY

1841
Birth of Pierre-Auguste Renoir at Limoges on 25 February.

1844
The Renoir family moves to Paris.

1854–8
Renoir is apprenticed to a porcelain painter in the rue des Fosses-du-Temple.

c. 1858–9
Earns a living by painting fans and blinds.

1860
Applies for a permit to make copies in the Louvre.

1862
Renoir is admitted to the École des Beaux-Arts and attends the studio of Gleyre.

1864
His painting *La Esmeralda* is accepted by the Salon.

1865
Exibits two paintings at the Salon, including a portrait of Sisley's father.

1866
One of Renoir's two submissions to the Salon is rejected and he withdraws the other. Renoir begins his liaison with Lise Tréhot.

1867
Diana (the Huntress) is rejected by the Salon. Renoir shares a studio with Bazille and Monet. He paints his first large picture out of doors.

1868
His portrait of Lise with an umbrella is exhibited at the Salon and draws some favourable comment.

1869
Paints with Monet at La Grenouillère. Has no money to buy paints.

1870
Exhibits the *Bather with Griffon* and the *Odalisque* at the Salon. After the outbreak of war Renoir is drafted and sent to Bordeaux, where he nearly dies of dysentery.

1871
In Paris during the Commune.

1872
Rejected at the Salon.

1873
Again rejected at the Salon. Introduced to the dealer Durand-Ruel.

1874
Takes part in the first group exhibition of the Impressionists.

1876
Exhibits 15 works in the Second Impressionist Exhibition including

Moulin de la Galette.

1877

Exhibits 21 works in the Third Impressionist Exhibition.

1879

Refuses to take part in the Fourth Impressionist Exhibition. Has first great success at the Salon with his Portrait of *Mme. Charpentier and her Children.*

1880

One again exhibits at the Salon and refuses to take part in the Fifth Impressionist Exhibition. Meets his future wife Aline Charigot.

1881

Travels to Algeria where he paints the *Arab Festival.* Paints *The Luncheon of the Boating Party* for which Aline Charigot poses. Travels to Italy where he is deeply impressed by the frescoes of Raphael and Pompeian wall paintings.

1882

Grudgingly takes part in Seventh Impressionist Exhibition.

1883

Durand-Ruel organizes a one-man show for Renoir which includes 70 works.

1885

Birth of his first son Pierre. Paints at La Roche-Guyon with Cézanne.

1886

Durand-Ruel shows 38 works by Renoir in New York. Renoir refuses to take part in the final Impressionist Exhibition.

1887

Exhibits the *Bather*, the most important work of his 'dry' period at the Galerie Georges Petit.

1890

Marries Aline Charigot. Exhibits for the last time at the Salon.

1892

French State buys *Young Girls at the Piano.* Durand-Ruel holds a Renoir retrospective which includes 110 works.

1894

After the death of Caillebotte, six paintings by Renoir from his collection are bequeathed to the Musée du Luxembourg. Birth of Renoir's second son Jean.

1895

Buys a house in his wife's native village of Essoyes.

1897

Breaks arm in a fall from a bicycle.

1900

Eleven paintings by Renoir are shown at the World Exhibition in Paris. Accepts the order of the 'Chevalier de la Légion d'honneur'.

1901

Birth of his third son Claude.

1902

Attacks of rheumatism become increasingly severe.

1904

A room is devoted to the works of Renoir at the Salon d'Automne.

1907

Buys the estate of Les Collettes at Cagnes and builds a house there. *Mme. Charpentier and her Children* acquired by the Metropolitan Museum in New York.

1910

Finally forced to give up walking.

1913

Five paintings by Renoir included in the Armory Show in New York. Renoir takes up sculpture with the help of Richard Guino.

1914

Renoir's sons Pierre and Jean are wounded in the First World War.

1915

Aline Renoir dies.

1919

Renoir is made a 'Commandeur de la Légion d'honneur'. Visits the Louvre for the last time. Completes his final masterpiece *The Bathers.* Dies on 3rd December.

LIST OF PLATES

27: Renoir, *Portrait of Richard Wagner*, Musée d'Orsay.

28: Renoir, *Washerwoman*, Durand Ruel Archives.

31: Degas, *After the Bath, Woman drying herself*, National Gallery, London.

32: Renoir, *Study of a Nude Woman*, Private Collection, Durand Ruel Archives.

33: Renoir, *Nude Woman*, red and white chalk drawing 1880–1890, British Museum (De Hanke Bequest).

35: Renoir with Andrée Hessling, wife of Jean Renoir, 1915, Durand Ruel Archives.

36: Renoir's house at Les Collettes, Cagnes.

37: Renoir and his family at Les Colletes, Cagnes, with his model, Gabrielle, on his left.

39: Renoir, *Venus Victorious*, 1914.

41: Renoir at Les Collettes, Cagnes.

44: *Portrait of Mademoiselle Romaine Lacaux*, 1864, oil on canvas, 81 × 64 cm. Cleveland Museum of Art, Cleveland, Ohio.

46: *Still Life*, 1864, oil on canvas, 130 × 98.4 cm. Kunsthalle, Hamburg.

48: *The Inn at Mother Anthony's*, 1866, oil on canvas, 193 × 130 cm. Nationalmuseum, Stockholm.

50: *Portrait of Bazille*, 1867, oil on canvas, 105 × 73.5 cm. Musée d'Orsay, Paris.

52: *Lise with a Parasol*, 1867, oil on canvas, 182 × 118 cm. Folkwang Museum, Essen.

54: *Diana (the Huntress)*, 1867, oil on canvas, 189 × 126 cm. National Gallery of Art, Washington (Chester Dale Collection).

56: *Portrait of M. and Mme. Sisley*, 1868, oil on canvas, 105 × 75 cm. Bridgeman Art Library, Wallraf-Richartz Museum, Cologne.

58: *La Grenouillère*, 1969, oil on canvas, 66 × 81 cm. Nationalmuseum, Stockholm.

60: *Flowers in a Vase*, c. 1869, oil on canvas, 64.9 × 54.2 cm. Museum of Fine Arts, Boston.

62: *Odalisque*, 1870, oil on canvas, 68.5 × 123 cm. National Gallery of Art, Washington. Chester Dale Collection.

64: *The Bather with Griffon*, 1870, oil on canvas, 184.2 × 114.9 cm. Museu de Arte, Sao Paulo.

66: *The Pont-Neuf*, 1872, oil on canvas, 75 × 92 cm. Ailsa Mellon Bruce Collection, National Gallery of Art, Washington.

68: *Riding in the Bois de Boulogne*, 1873, oil on canvas, 261 × 226 cm. Bridgeman Art Library, Kunsthalle, Hamburg.

70: *Portrait of Monet*, 1875, oil on canvas, 85 × 60.5 cm. Musée d'Orsay, Paris.

72: *The Gust of Wind*, c. 1873, oil on canvas, 52 × 82.5 cm. Fitzwilliam Museum, Cambridge.

74: *Mme. Claude Monet with her Son*. 1874, oil on canvas, 50.4 × 68 cm. Ailsa Mellon Bruce Collection, National Gallery of Art, Washington.

76: *La Loge*, 1874, oil on canvas, 80 × 64 cm, Courtauld Collection, Courtauld Institute Galleries, London.

78: *Self-Portrait*, 1875, oil on canvas, 39.1 × 31.7 cm. Sterling and Francine Clark Art Institute, Williamstown, Mass.

80: *Portrait of M. Chocquet*, 1876, oil on canvas, 47 × 37 cm. Fogg Art Museum, Harvard University, Cambridge, Mass. Bequest of Grenville Winthrop.

82: *Nude in the Sunlight*, 1876, oil on canvas, 81 × 64.8 cm. Musée d'Orsay, Paris.

84: *The Swing*, 1876, oil on canvas, 92 × 73 cm. Bridgeman Art Library, Musée d'Orsay, Paris.

86: *Moulin de la Galette*, 1876, oil on canvas, 130 × 175 cm. Musée d'Orsay, Paris.

88: *The First Outing*, 1876, oil on canvas, 65 × 50 cm. National Gallery, London.

90: *Garden in the rue Cortot, Montmartre*, 1876, oil on canvas, 151.8 × 97.5 cm. Museum of Art, Carnegie Institute, Pittsburg.

92: *Woman with Umbrella and Child*, 1877, oil on canvas, 46 × 55 cm. Museum of Fine Arts, Boston, Mass.

94: *Mme. Charpentier and her Children*, 1878, oil on canvas, 153.7 × 190.2 cm. Metropolitan Museum of Art, Wolfe Fund, 1907, Catherine Lonilard Wolfe Collection, New York.

96: *The Skiff*, c. 1879, oil on canvas, 71 × 92 cm. National Gallery, London.

98: *Portrait of Mlle. Irène Cahen d'Anvers*, 1880, oil on canvas, 64 × 54 cm. Foundation E.G. Burhle Collection, Zurich.

100: *The Luncheon of the Boating Party*, 1880–1, oil on canvas, 130 × 175.5 cm. Phillips Collection, Washington.

102: *Blond Bather*, 1881, oil on canvas, 81.8 × 65.7 cm. Sterling and Francine Clark Art Institute, Williamstown, Mass.

104: *Arab Festival*, 1881, oil on canvas, 72 × 92 cm. Musée d'Orsay.

106: *Still Life with Onions*, 1881, oil on canvas, 39.1 × 60.6 cm. Sterling and Francine Clark Art Institute, Williamstown, Mass.

108: *The Umbrellas*, c. 1881–5, oil on canvas, 180 × 115 cm. National Gallery, London.

110: *Portrait of Charles and Georges Durand-Ruel*, 1882, oil on canvas, 65 × 81 cm. Collection Durand-Ruel, Paris.

112: *Dance at Bougival*, 1882–3, oil on canvas, 180 × 98 cm. Museum of Fine Arts, Boston.

114: *Portrait of Paul Haviland*, 1884, oil on canvas, 57 × 43 cm. Nelson-Atkins Museum of Art, Kansas City, Missouri.

116: *The Children's Afternoon at Wargemont*, 1884, oil on canvas, 127

× 173 cm. Bildarchiv Preussischer Kulturbesitz, Berlin.

118: *La Roche-Guyon*, *c.* 1885, oil on canvas, 48 × 55.5 cm. Aberdeen Art Gallery and Museum.

120: *The Large Bathers*, 1887, oil on canvas, 115 × 170 cm. Philadelphia Museum of Art.

122: *Bather Arranging her Hair*, 1887, oil on canvas, 40 × 31 cm. National Gallery, London.

124: *Young Girls at the Piano*, 1892, oil on canvas, 112 × 99 cm. Musée d'Orsay.

126: *Gabrielle with Jean*, *c.* 1900, oil on canvas, 65 × 54 cm. Bridgeman Art Library, Musée de l'Orangerie, Paris.

128: *Sleeping Woman*, 1897, oil on canvas, 80 × 62 cm. Oskar Reinhart Collection, Am Römerholz Winterthur.

130: *Portrait of Misia Edwards*, 1906, oil on canvas, 80 × 62 cm. National Gallery, London.

132: *Portrait of Ambroise Vollard*, 1908, oil on canvas, 81 × 64 cm. Courtauld Collection, Courtauld Institute Galleries London.

134: *The Clown*, 1909, oil on canvas, 120 × 77 cm. Musée de l'Orangerie, Collection Walter-Guillaume, Paris.

136: *Mme. Renoir with her Dog Bob*, *c.* 1910, oil on canvas, 81 × 65 cm. Wadsworth Atheneum, Hartford, Conn.

138: *The Bathers*, *c.* 1918–19, oil on canvas, 110 × 160 cm. Bridgeman Art Library, Musée d'Orsay.